THE
PASSION
OF
A
POET

A PAINFUL REALITY

By Author Harvey Howell
&
Co-Author Shamika Gray

authorHOUSE®

AuthorHouse™
1663 Liberty Drive
Bloomington, IN 47403
www.authorhouse.com
Phone: 1 (800) 839-8640

Published by AuthorHouse 12/06/2018

ISBN: 978-1-5462-0713-9 (sc)
ISBN: 978-1-5462-0712-2 (e)

Library of Congress Control Number: 2017913698

Print information available on the last page.

This book is printed on acid-free paper.

Contents

Acknowledgements

I want to first thank our one true rabb and only lord of mankind and all that exist. I thank him for my creation. I thank him for my abilities and sanity. For waking up another day and for realizing that my life has great purpose. I would also like to thank him for my vision to see life through different perspectives. Without him nothing is possible not even life itself. I would also like to thank a few people who believed in me and saw something great when I didn't see the potential in myself. Thank you, mom for being the woman you are and never neglecting me. My Aunty Sheila McDonald for always wanting what was best for me and for me to live positively. My two beautiful number one supporters, Pamela and Rekyra Berry. Thank you for helping me find my passion. Elizabeth Lopez, and Christine Brown. Thank you all for believing in me and seeing that I could be more than a product influenced by my environment. Thank you for your strength and advice. And for having faith that I can turn temporary defeat into success.

I want to thank my brother's Jerome Howell and Willie Green for encouraging me to pursue a better path and being my reason for change. Willie, I know I haven't set a good example to follow, but I'm proud that you made better choices with your life than I have. And I wish to only make you as proud with the decisions I make from here on out. I want to credit a few good friends and family who helped me along the way with this book. Those who provided me with insightful information, helped with research, or contributed to some of the concepts I use which inspired some of these poems. To my brother in faith and dear friend Jamel Leonard, I thank you for your input and advice and want you to know that there's many mountains that hinders people's path but, with the ambition you have you'll always find a way to reach your designated goal. To Hasaan Shipman aka short leg, thank you for your thoughts which helped increase my ideals for this book. Thank you for challenging me and my creativeness and showing me that I can accomplish anything I put my mind to. To Xavier Villanueva, thank you for helping me with the visualization for the cover of the book and for being patient with me and a brother. You honestly helped me reach deeper into myself at times to bring these poems to life.

I want to thank the women in my life who has also been amazing with their support and contribution to my completion of this book, such as Melonie Greene. Thank you for your warm heart, your assistance, your devotion, and being a great friend when I needed one. To Monique Neysmith, thank you for always being authentic and helping me see the changes I needed to make within myself. Thank you for never turning your back on me even when I displayed the poorest quality of character. Thanks for being the most genuine friend I have Moe. And to Shanika Grey, thank you for your bountiful efforts, sacrifices, your expertise, partnership and encouragement. Thank you for all that you've been to me and all that you are to me. Thank you for providing me with a family I can rely on and a family I can call my own. But most of all thank you for my son Juelz. To Chanel Johnson, thank you for being the sister I needed. Thank you for being that light of hope for my brother and staring him clear from the dreadful path. Thank you for your help and making this book a success and my beautiful nieces and nephew.

Thank you, Uncle Willie and Author Lee, for being everything my Aunt and mother has ever desired. Thank you both for being real men and never abandoning your responsibilities. Thank you for showing me what a man supposed to represent and how much family is important.

My prayers, gratitude, an appreciation goes out to the readers who took their time to invest in my thoughts. Those who can identify with my writings and relate to these concepts. I pray for the best for you and hope that I've provided something that could be of some kind of benefit to you, a family member, or a friend life. I wish to make mention that readers should have an open mind when reading about some of the topics this book pertains. And I would like for readers to know that it's not in my intention to insult anyone, anybody, or any particular group. these poems are not to single out, ridicule, or target any person

I apologize beforehand if anyone takes offense to the contents of the subject matters. they are only opinionated views that I wanted to touch on and give readers a piece of mind to dwell on

Special shout out to Jermal Clemons "swage" S.C, Stacy "Bklyn" Tompkins P.S Keith Mahatha "lench" N.C, Antonio Nicholson "LA" N.C, Jahid "Brian" Baltimore M.D, Antonie Pope "hakeem" N.Y, James Sessoms "popsi" N.Y, Tafari Richardson "tee" N.Y, Kabir aka Cromratie bka Brownsville Da hill dats real white walls jets, "L.O" N.Y, "Lust" N.Y, Stevie medina P.A, Jamal Brown "Mal-g" N.Y, Henry Medina "Snoop" N.Y, Harmeil Shamblee "higs" N.Y, Michael Burmundez "Jizz" N.Y, Derrick Jackson "d-bo" N.Y, Jonny reeves "Hard" RIP N.Y, and Steve James "chip" C.C uptown.

But I would like to give big thanks and send my love to all those I may have forgotten. I'll try to make up for it in my next book, God willingly.

To my supporters,

You've been there through the good and the bad and tough times that had me doubting myself. The struggles that had me contemplating giving up. You reassured me time after time that I can achieve anything I put my mind too. That failure is just a figment of my imagination. And only when I've stopped trying is when I failed myself. You've supportive through the hardship I endured and let me know that as long as I have life in me I still have the will to achieve my endeavors and the ability to keep trying to rebuild my circumstances I'm hindered by. You gave me hope when I lost faith and became despaired by my trials and impediments. You saw my potential before I even realized I could do or be anything I wanted to be. You been nothing but inspirational and encouraging to me. And my success is truly because of you. I thank you for all you have done for me and all you have been to me. And now I understand the reason you have always been successful in your endeavors because you weren't selfish in your desires for other people success as well. May you live long, accomplished everything you hoped for, and truly receive endless blessings. thank you.

To my doubters,

They say hate is a poisonous disease that better the soul. It corrupts the heart to breed envy for those who wish to obtain greatness. The people who strive for what they believe in, upset you to the point their success makes you unhappy. You can't stand the fact that others are determined to bring their dream to fruition. But it's not the intention of anyone to offend you by chasing their goals. And it's not meant for their success to anger you. Your failure to prosper cause you to resent others being that you haven't accomplished your desires. And I understand. Life can be difficult for us all. But you can't fault others for your shortcomings. I believe that one day you'll make it if you focus your energy on productive matters, yourself and continue strive. I believe that you'll prevail even if you feel different about me. To be successful, you must think successfully. And success to me is hoping that we all succeed.

So, to my doubters, I want you to know that you've been the fuel that feeds my passion. And I thank you because without you I wouldn't have had the strength or ambition that pushes me. I wouldn't have been able to prove to myself or those who believe in me that I can make it.

Every great dream begins with a dreamer. Always remember, you have within you the strength, the patience, and the passion to reach for the stars to change the world.

-Harriet Tubman

Introduction

Before I even had the thought or idea of doing a poem book I used to occasionally write poems for a few special individuals in my life. It was something I did to show them how important they were to me. My writings were always personal, kept myself, or shared with those I loved at the time. It wasn't until two special women in my life by the name of Pamela Berry and Elizabeth Lopez had encouraged me after heavy pleading to write a book. Pamela used to tell me how she would frame my poems and hang them on the wall by the front door in her home, and how everyone who walked through her door would read the poems I had personally sent to her and inquired who I was or when I was coming out with a book. So, you can imagine how pressured I became by Pamela from then on. And as you can see she finally got through to me after all of her persisting persuasion. Elizabeth use to question me about my creativeness to write and inquire why I didn't produce a book that inspires people like the poems I often would send her to brighten her mood. After reading this you will come to know that these are not the kind of poems she had in mind. But I'm working on three more poem books in addition to this one that will become a series. When I started my mission to write a poem book, I thought I'd just write several poems and just put them out. It wasn't until my vision took on a life of its own that I figured my poems deserved a breakdown which is a broader explanation and interpretation of what my poems represent. I wanted to do something different than other poets that would show the passion from where my thoughts derived. Or the meaning of what's intended as my expressions. And as I wrote my vision for my poetry started to expand. This first book which is titled passion of a poet, is the actual name of the book but this version is called "A Painful Reality" because of the disappointment or harsh views that's being addressed. I gave some of the poems a secondary elucidation in addition to the breakdowns because of the facts or necessary research I wanted to implement that was very informative and significant to what I was trying to convey. My passion for writing is profound. And in my passion, there's pain, concerns, inspiration and love. It's the good and poor concepts that shows a point from various angles in all the above categories. I wanted to first show the painful views of the harsh existence that most experience which, is a painful reality for all of us. Not just those suffering from it. There are four additions to this book and I wanted this version to be the first one I put out because I wanted to voice the issues that burdens us all. The issues that may not be questioned enough. The things which makes us feel victimized or responsible. Judged by different standards of morality. I wanted readers to see the hurt that others endure, experience or evoke. The hurt they may feel they can relate too. And the actions that earn other's complaints or disapproval. This is the pain I express through my passion in this book.

But as I was saying, that's when my vision begin to inhance, and I got an idea to not only include the interpretation of my thoughts so that the concepts is even more meaningful, but to also write four different compilations of poetic expressions to identify with several matters. The second version to this book will be called "Where there's reason to wonder". The third vision is "From the passion within", that will be about the inspirational things and just the passion I possess. And the fourth version will be called "Expectations of love".

While writing this book I was being relocated to South Carolina from New Hampshire. During the process I end up losing one of my poem books (which was dropped off somewhere down in South Carolina upon my transition) that I had intended to use for this series of poem books. I remember trying to do everything I can possibly do to get it back. But to no avail, I was left feeling like it just wasn't meant to be. The person who ended up receiving my book ended up calling my aunt Sheila McDonald to return the book being that a copy of my phone book was also in the package that contained my book. At first upon hearing the news I was relieved and grateful. But once I realized that it was just a lousy attempt of Noble character on the persons behalf

I became discouraged and almost gave up because I felt that it had some of my best work. My aunt was the one who advised me to keep going and provided me with the motivation I needed to continue my goal. She was the one who insisted that I keep pursuing my desire to express this passion for poetry I have within me. I thought back to when I was in middle school and a teacher once told me that I had something truly special and if I continued to work at it, one day I would really do something extraordinary. Back then I gave up on the idea of writing and lost myself in the streets. I had a habit of not adhering to advice that was meant with good intention. I didn't want to give up on myself or the people who believed in me anymore. So, I wrote other poems to make up for the lack thereof and tried to recapture some of the ones I sort of remembered. I have to say that I am fortunate and grateful that I had that encouragement from my aunt. It made me see that I have within me the ability to create another book and what's come to pass shouldn't be dwelled on to cause further discouragement. And I'm proud that I had the help of everyone else who made this possible for me. This is The Passion of a Poet: A Painful Reality. I truly hope that you enjoy the way I articulate these perspectives.

The conversation: Incertitude

(elder) what's up young blood, why don't you tell me how you living?,

(youth) well you know me old "G" surviving by any means I see befitting,

(elder) so is that the motto you follow which assures everything you do with conviction?,

(youth) Nah! But it's the reality I'm led to believe due to the foul conditions we live in,

(elder) So your telling me your actions are justified by the circumstances you been given?,

(youth) I mean; it's the only way to perceive it when opportunities aren't presented,

(elder) So I assume you actually tried; or is that statement based off opinions?,

(youth) Honestly; why should I make any attempt when the obvious is clearly convincing?,

(elder) Because nothing should be expected if the effort isn't intended,

And those who aren't persistent make excuses for a poor existence,

(youth) But what about those who righteously strove to advance and still encountered resistance?,

1

(elder) Not every challenge is going to be fair; nor could all ignorance be prevented,

(youth) Then how is it possible to stay determined when the odds are stacked against us?,

(elder) By facing every disadvantage with confidence and ambition,

(youth) But regardless of good intentions still we're viewed as violent offenders,

(elder) Which is the reason you should believe in yourself despite those who perceive you different,

Do you think those before you who accumulated success were repelled by opposition?,

Or let impediments hinder their mission and kept them from achieving their acquisition?,

(youth) No! But how much sacrifice is required in order to make an ordinary living?,

(elder) As much as needed or necessary to enable a successful transition,

(youth) I understand you clearly, but I just think wishful thinking is for the optimistic,

(elder) I mean your entitled to feel any way you please

But honestly you should give more thought to the path you choose before making a life changing decision,

Because second chances aren't offered, and most choices doesn't lead to the most favorable ending we envision.

P.O.A.P

The Conversation: Incertitude

THE BREAK DOWN

This poem is about a conversation between an elder guy in the young man who converse about the choices that could affect this young guy greatly. The choices that could determine a positive or negative outcome. And the life changing volition that could alter one path or liberty. In this conversation you will see a dialogue which convey a concept of the type of discussion that would usually take place between these two individuals. The advice that's given and the responses which question one's theory. I wanted to articulate something that everybody goes through in their life. I believe that everyone has made a mistake in their life that they regret. A mistake that could have been avoided if they had just taken heed to the advice they were given. I wanted to show the doubts or uncertainty many young adults have about their purpose in life. And relate why most young men choose the streets instead of a more legitimate way of living. I wanted to show the conversation that takes place, as many does, when a young person is on the wrong path and is admonished by an elder who wish to intercede so that the young man doesn't make the same mistakes he once made. In this poem I would like for the readers to assume that the older guy is aware of the decisions that young male face. But he's been down this road before and is familiar with the results of making the wrong choices. You can even imagine that this younger person is you, and you were being lectured by an older guy who recognize your potential and just wish for you to make the right choices. I wanted to create something mostly all people can identify with. This is The Conversation Incertitude.

In the first line I want to show just the basic introduction between the elder in the young man. I wanted this greeting to give an ideal of their familiarity with each other. I wanted it to show the elders concerned with a young guys wellbeing. He inquires to know how he's managing, which tells the reader that he genuinely cares about this kid. And the young man response back by acknowledging the elder as an "O.G" which is the sign of respect and honor in the streets "O.G" which means original gangster, is only attributed to those who lived a glorified lifestyle. I further intended to show how close these two individuals were and how much respect was held. That one could see the young man's extensive response is a bit perplexing and immature. He feels that he has no choice but to survive by any means that suit him. Whatever is necessary for him to maintain he is willing to do regardless of the consequence or risk. So, the elder man questions if he truly believes that kind of mentality is going to guarantee him success. The young man slightly hesitates by starting his reply with nah. It shows that he's not certain if he should believe it or not, but he feels it's the reality he is forced to believe due to his circumstances. Most young men think that there's no hope for them. They think that there is no other way to make a successful living without resorting to miscreant ways. They think that people like them only have one option because the conditions their in. For most, all they know are things they grow up to see that affirms what they should look forward to or expect out of life. To hope to become anything more than what's been the result of their environment is honestly unrealistic for them. They feel pressured by society to fail because of a botch hand the were dealt. But like most elders who see great quality in our youth, this guy in this conversation is no different. He's disappointed that this young man is actually trying to use this situation as an excuse. That he's already allowing himself to be defeated because he's placed in an unfortunate predicament. But the young man obstinacy prevents him from seeing his own advantages or accountability. The benefits that makes him aware of the stakes and what he's up against. And the accountability of realizing that failure can only be obtained by giving up on oneself.

The young man feels that the lack of opportunities is enough reason for him to consider other avenues of monetary gain. Since he isn't presented many options, he automatically develops a state of pessimism and except the worst possibility he could choose for himself. A possibility that guarantees more devastation than gratification. But it seems he is willing to ruin his life rather than to struggle to make a decent living.

Most young men choose to adopt the street code without even making an attempt to pursue a lawful path. They don't give much thought or effort to a legitimate pursuit and often find themselves caught up in a terrible situation. The elderly man questions the youths effort to make a difference by inquiring what options have this young man exhausted? What alternatives did he take? Did he even try? Or is his perception based off the opinion other's may have influenced him with?

The young man makes it clear that, it's not the views of other's which have him thinking this way. It's his view of the world and the impression society has given him. The impression that he will end up a failure. The indication that he would never surmount the challenging obstacles ahead. Some young men believe that the reality they perceive is a projection of the adversity they will suffer also, being that they identify or share a resemblance to the people who struggles they witness. So, if the world shows the history of black people being treated as if their worthless, then how could they assume that their lives matter? But the older man wants him to know that nothing could be expected out of life if one doesn't apply themselves. And that only people who aren't willing to commit to a purpose are the ones who make excuses for their "poor" existence. If one view the world with the same expectations that were afforded to others, they wouldn't amount to anything more than what's surmised by their assumptions.

The young man believes that regardless if he pursued the right course of direction or not, people like him are still treated no differently from a criminal. He points out the fact that there are people who strove righteously who have still ended up in a "poor" state. People who have lived honestly and labored in a just manner. So why shouldn't he live violently or distribute narcotics and conform to the misconceptions or stereotypes? Why should it matter how he lives his life when either way he chooses, he still could end up with problems or faced with hardship? And though his intentions may be good his worries would still be the same. Why should he strive in such a correct manner only to suffer or be denied fair consideration? Why should he wish to pursue a righteous path when the odds against black people are stacked? How is it possible for him or anyone else to stay determined under such conditions?

The elder try to bring to his attention that there may be opposing elements of life everyone meets. He believes that the way we're viewed should make us wish to change any misconstruction about us. And show those who misjudge us that we can be better than what they equate to us. There will always be obstructions that serve to impede or suppress one's ability to excel in life. And it will not always be fair or justified. They will not always turn out the way we desire. Sometimes it will be ignorant people who deprive others of their endeavors or set goals. People who stand in the way of other's prosperity because of their aversion. But by staying persistent and facing every disadvantage with confident ambition, we can prevail over any situation even if we're viewed with senseless hatred. No matter the difficulty one should always believe in his/her self and not allow anything or no one to cause them to have doubt in their ability to flourish.

The people the elder guy was referring to that accumulated success despite being repelled by opposition is referring to Dr. Martin Luther King Jr., Rosa Parks, Nelson Mandela, Malcolm X and all the other successful black people that paved their way and achieved what they set out to obtain regardless of those who tried to hinder them. Those who taught us how to be brave and have confidence. Those who showed us how to humble ourselves and fight for what we believe in. He wanted the young man to know that they didn't give in to opposition. That they didn't gain their victories by settling for the worse possibility. Or allowed impediments to suppress their mission.

The young man shows that he is conscious of the sacrifices it took for him to have his independence of choice. And the lives that were taken in order for him to be afforded greater opportunities. He actually views every sacrificed made as if it was his own. But he wanted to know how much more do him or anyone have to endure just to live an ordinary life? Just to be free of any contention? Although this young man believes he has the power to strive, he refuses to take a chance due to the odds working against him.

The elder lets him know that he should be willing to make as many sacrifices as necessary in order to change the reality we suffer from. Sometimes it requires much dedication to make the most productive living we desire. And sometimes we are going to be trial with great tribulation but, we must have faith that we will rise. That we will be successful in our pursuit.

This young man has seen so much that he's become despaired at the thought of trying. He's seen his parents break their backs. He's seen those close to him struggle only to be overlooked or undervalued. He feels that believing things will ever change is wishful thinking, and he's refused to die in vain.

Although the elder knows he's entitled to his feelings, he understands that second chances aren't offered. He wants what is best for him. He doesn't want the young man to regret his decisions later on down the road. He sees the potential in this young man he didn't see in himself at that young age. He warns him to give more thought to the path he takes in life. And informs him that without hope, his feelings or views on things will only be pessimistic. The elder man knows that this young man fate is inevitable and for the first time realized that his stubbornness was more familiar than he'd thought.

Wake Up

The streets and its glory they say,

Fascinated by the wicked things that enhance the stories they relay,

The stories of the greats that died or is confined to a four by four eating three hot's in a two-cot cell with one door,

Counting down their regrets like a release date,
Reflecting on moments of guilt wishing they could have change their fate,

But life's test only requires one take,
Taken by temptation that beautifies the urges of desire; So that many can't resist the bait,

Especially when it's encouraged by those we idolize who assist in leading us astray,

But we insist by believing that's the way,

Sleep walking cause we're blind followers in a comatose state repeating the same mistakes,

Unaware of the mendacious display,
The material illusions which makes us pretentious,
Allured by the acquisitive that captures our interest,

And when finances are pending it's hard to have faith that's convincing,

And in god we trust but the bible they study is green with big faces that finance their incentive,

But religion could be offensive to those who are sacrilegious; Or maybe it's the other way around depending what devotion is intended,

But the notion that's presented is that the mind doesn't focus unless notice is brought to our attention,

So, wake up to a purpose and stop dozing off on the mission.

P.O.A.P

Wake Up

THE BREAK DOWN

This poem is about the fallacious conception that is presented by miscreants, delinquents or those living in error who filcher the innocence of young teenagers or those who are swindled by illusions. Illusions of a life that is magnified by wealth, material possessions, and passion. It's the illusion's that are exaggerated by those who thrive to corrupt other's through manipulation or persuasion. I wanted to convey a message that would grant clarity in the wake of uncertainty when there's doubt about the facades we are mesmerized by. The things that causes us to stray from a righteous path. When the artificial appearance which seems fulfilling, tempts our desires. It's a slight calling for us to wake up consciously and stop sleeping on the problems we face that are devitalizing.

The streets have many tales. Tales that are adventurous, exciting, lavishing, and desirable. There are also tales of horrific accounts as well but, it's often glorified by the things that fascinate us most. Things that incite the urge to pursue the same acquisition. The stories that eulogize the dead or magnify the "lifestyle" of those who have given their lives to the streets. Relayed by the people who assist in this despondent cycle of misconceptions and pipe dreams.

These stories aren't told over a camp fire or presented as fables and myths for entertainment during forest or outside dwellings. There more factual than fictitious and are intended to influence malefaction. They are narratives of the "greats" who lived rhapsodic in their corrupt ways. The "greats" who are considered legendary by those who follow cluelessly in perversion. These stories are always highlighted by their conquest or luxury but never by their consequences or outcomes. It's never emphasized that these "greats" are no longer living because they were brutally gunned down or is now confined to a four by four (which is a cell) eating three hots' in a two-cot cell with one door. This expression is to stress what a person who breaks the law must look forward to. The four by four is not only a reference to a cell but, it's also the length of time one may be subject to. As in 4X4, which is 16 years. It's also a clever way I used to show the regretful mistakes inmates dwell on while counting down their jail time till the day of their release. These regrets are something they live with till the end of their sentence term. Moments of guilt that is reflected upon daily. The guilt they wish they could change along with the choice they've made that cost them their freedom. Most people aren't told about this part of the story. They aren't told that you only get one take during life's test. And changing your fate after choosing an illegal path isn't something that's granted. It isn't something that those "greats" were provided or non to come would be rendered.

These illusions are beautified in the most appealing manner. They excite our desires so much that we can't resist the urge to seek such pleasures even if those pleasures are unwholesome. We become taken by the bait of temptation that lure us into a trap. The bait which is set up by those we idolize who encourage our failure by leading us astray by giving erroneous advice. But we often insist in the advice we're receiving by believing in this faultiness of error. We allow ourselves to be misled by not taking heed to the results of the tales.

We're blind followers in a comatose state. A state of deep unconsciousness because of a mental disease that impairs our ability to think. Blindly following the mistakes of other's as if we're asleep and unaware of the reality of what has come to pass. Or unobservant of the false display or mendacious show of extravagance that is pleasing to the eyes. Like jewelry, clothes, cars and promiscuous women, which makes us ambitious to attain a certain condition. Demanding to possess the image we perceive that attracts our interest. And lure us in by the objective we wish to acquire.

It's generally known that most people living in urban ghettos or poverty restricted areas aren't as fortunate as other's. We're living in low income communities that are pressured by society to live a certain way in order to escape the embarrassment and shame of not having. When you take that into consideration along with the humiliation of not wanting to be the individual family who stands out as the most impecunious, out of all the people in the same unfortunate predicament that may have a little more structure then you, that may further aggrandize insult by making you feel more worthless than you already feel. So, when one's manhood is tested we seem to think that sacrificing ourselves in order to live is a necessity. And when finances like bills, food, shelter, and clothing is pending it's hard to have faith that you'll come out of poor circumstances economically or socially.

And even though we trust in god it's hard not to study the function of money when it's constantly flaunted by other's. And after a while the ideal of having, is enough to finance your actions to procure wealth even if the path isn't suitable. And when pursuing money in any illegal manner, it weighs down on the conscience of those who are god fearing. Those who acknowledge the laws god decreed but has neglected them. And those who have faith but has become sacrilegious because of their disobedience. It would offend anybody who is living in error when religion is brought up just as it would offend those who are religious when they must witness a condemnatory act of transgression. It depends on which way the devotion is driven but it's always going to be offensive to all in the matter of right or wrong. But the concept that's understood is that the mind won't see a clear picture if a thought isn't brought to our attention. Meaning that we can't see that our paths are misguided when we don't have people to point out our mistakes. Sometimes we are so invested into a thing that we become oblivious to everything else.

So, wake up to a purpose, a goal, a plan, or a righteous cause. And stop dozing off on the mission to be something better, someone successful, or a positive influence.

Black Man Why I Hate My Self

Mirror – mirror on the wall who is the most racist people of them all?,

It was a short pause as the mirror begins to fog and an image appeared before my eyes which begin to talk,

There is none with greater hate then the African American or as most say Black color people these days,

The mirror replied as I stirred through the eyes of my own reflection,

Lend me your ear said the depiction in the mirror before me as I listened in eagerly to receive the message,

Though it's not a different race it's your own your rejecting,

Turning your back on your brother's and sister's,

Thinking your any different because you've be giving a position,

Adopting a porch nigger's mentality; Then it's apparent you're the only one who fails to see the actual reality,

Pushing away the innocence that lies within; rather kill – betray – and steal from each other instead of providing a helping hand,

Taught to hate yourself by this cruel society; deceive – cheat – and mislead one another to perceive that which is wrong is right; deluding most people of their chance to make it out of poverty without supplying drugs or resorting to robbery,

Your ancestors fought diligently and adamantly for you to live freely,

But instead your miscreant ways cause you to be caged like animals and viewed ignorantly,

Unable to break out of the slave mentality; so, you violate laws constantly becoming criminals or low life individuals in servility; I mean servitude facilities were slavery still exit undeniably,

So black man why is it that you hate yourself I ask?,

Because; you like others wasn't given a chance,

Because of the color of your skin complexion your judged before the greeting of hands with just a glance,

Hated by other's so you develop that same hatred towards your own sister's and brother's almost as if it's a trend,

Quick to turn on your own kind to prove that your different when your every bit the same outside on the surface and within,

All your life you've been afflicted with pain; from being enslaved to your ancestor's being whipped,

From being maimed; till this day black people are still being lynched,

So how could you hate yourself black man when those of your own race are suffering from the same evils you are up against?,

Is what the mirror mentions.

P.O.A.P

Black Man Why I Hate Myself

PART 1

THE BREAK DOWN

In this poem I wanted to show a black man in search of himself. I wanted to show a man looking to find answers within himself as to why he has experienced so much hatred or contributed to the hatred his people feels. It's actually a subliminal message to the black culture and how we've come to inherit the same hate we've been afflicted with. A lot of people make excuses to why they're in a predicament or why they are dealing with such circumstances. They never look at themselves as the source of their culpability. I wanted to show a man face to face with his own reflection who points out his worst enemy which is the self-image. I wanted to be able to relate through that reflection that most people assumption as to why their facing such issues becomes the reason to find fault in everything other than themselves. Sometimes when a thing has been in a condition for so long it becomes immune. It adapts the ways of the state it was in to the point it becomes a normal reality.

I was thinking of a way to show a man in thought. To show a person face to face with himself to question the cause of his reality. The most common place you would examine yourself for any blemishes or defects would be a mirror which is the reason I placed this character in a setting where he can inspect the thing he search for from a personal stand point. I wanted to give that fairy tale visual where the mirror begins to fog or produce smoke fumes right before the image appear. I wanted to capture the reader's imagination while conveying an essential message.

15

I wanted to make clear that it's not another race who have the most hatred towards black people as would be expected by someone who is face-to-face with themselves. It's the person before the mirror. It's the questioner themselves who has been confronted by their own awareness. It's almost as if being in a spot light. Feeling like you could depend on the one person you know who would cosign what you believe only to have them point out your error's.

Even though the self-image is disgusted with the awareness one may perceive, it is always willing to make the conscious apparent of the actual nature of things. As long as one is willing to take heed or gain understanding, only then it can correct the way the mind view things.

It's known that racism is when another race feels superior and discriminate against another race because of that, this racism that is expressed towards its own race of people is no different. In some cases, you have black people who have separated themselves so much from their own identity that they honestly believe that they share no likeness with other black people especially those of lesser conditions or circumstances. It's made clear that rejecting or turning on our own brother's and sister's is something that is unacceptable but, has been happening. There is no unity with in the black communities how there is in other groups. The support, aid, or help isn't something that comes naturally with black people. That genuine desire to see their brothers or sisters ascend or become better in this life isn't a sincere consistency. We are more divided than any other race because of the lack of identifying with our self-image. 'self" meaning those who share the same reflection.

Those black people that do tend to think that there any different from others are mostly those in any kind of position or higher status to uplift their people but, instead look down on them as if there any better. They're the ones who look at their own race as a disgrace or repulsion instead of making a difference. They've become so content with their life styles that their determined to show a distinction between them and other blacks just to be accepted by a society who views them the same regardless of their distance from reality. They've adopted a porch nigger mentality because of this. A porch nigger was always known throughout time to be the characteristics of a black person who thought he was more of value or better than the rest because he felt he was more trusted by those who were oppressing his own kind. So, he made it his business to show his distinction by being only mindful of himself and over seeing his brother's and sister's slave conditions. It's apparent that these black people with that kind of mentality are the only one who doesn't notice their betrayal and ostracism from their own race. Everyone sees their disloyalty and aloofness from their own kind but them self.

I wanted to also address or direct something more towards the street individuals who indulge in everything non-productive or criminal. Giving the illusion to the younger generation that what they're doing is a credible way of living. Their pushing away the innocence of the youth by pulling them closer to a consequential fate. African Americans are more likely to be victimized by crime than any other group or people. This creates a set of individual and community problems which impede upon other areas of productive activities. Rather than provide a helping hand and build our people up it seems like violence towards one another has become an intentional objective. It's as if we would rather destroy ourselves than to cultivate our own race. It's like how we could critique another race for being racist when the hate we display towards our own kind is far worse. How could we complain about the discrimination against us when we treat our own brother's and sister's the cruelest? Rather kill – betray – and steal is not only referring to the deaths, dishonorable acts, or materialistic possession one may commit against another. It's also hinting at the lack of motivation – the deception of presenting a false reality – and abstractedly swiping one's hope.

This society we live in has been very malefic and cruel to black people since the beginning of slavery. It has been full of suffering, grief and affliction as we know. Only difference between now and then is that black people are the ones who are responsible for the misery and pain they cause themselves. It's almost like we adopted the iniquitous behaviors and heinous misconduct that has caused us great affliction. As if by going through such cruelty taught us how to be cruel to each other.

I wanted to discuss the issue of false guidance provided by those caught up in a criminal life style again. To me these individuals are the worse of human beings. Instead of showing young black men a better way, their misleading them to believe that the path they're on is correct. Giving them false hope in something that continues to destroy their lives and dreams. And cheating them out of a chance to become someone important or make a life for themselves. In some states, black men have been admitted to prison on drug charges at rates of twenty to fifty time greater than those of white men, as many as 80% of young African American men now have criminal records.

Sometimes it seems like we don't recognize how far we came as black people. And I wanted to remind our people what it took to get here. How much we endured to get to this point. How much strength was devoted or how much blood, sweat, and tears it took for our people to achieve such great victory. How much was sacrificed for us to live freely and no longer be oppressed or treated so maliciously. Only to go backwards. Only to be the ones who cause such affliction to one another. Honestly look at how far we came only to place ourselves back in a similar situation from which we rose from. How could we go against everything our ancestors stood for? How could we return to those shackles and binds after everything that has happened for us to gain our freedom? How ignorant can we actually be? Would we rather be treated like animals? Would we rather be viewed as such?

It seems like we have developed the slave mentality that once was. The mentality in which we believe we are better suited as slaves in servitude. The mentality that is hopeless and feels it serves no purpose to the life here in America. We continue to break laws that confine us to institutions or facilities as if we do not wish to be free. Prisons which are like slave plantations due to its servile conditions and controlled environment. The foul treatment as if you're no longer a human being. The pennies for labor and poor meals that's served. The prevention of being or interacting with your family in a functionally manner. Why become what was so desperately changed? Why go back to those conditions? Three out of four young black men (and nearly all those in poorest neighborhoods) can expect to serve time in prison.

I wanted to have people take an introspection of themselves. I wanted them to question their actions. It's a general inquisition to all black people out there that seem to be dedicated to the destruction of our own race. Why is it that you hate you own kind? Your own self-image. "Self-image" meaning your color or complexion. Your race of people.

It's apparent that black Americans are the most discriminated race. Their deprived of opportunities and chances before their even considered. In many events due to the color of our skin, black people are judged before the greeting of hands. We are judged before introducing ourselves. We are judged before a person get the chance to know us personally. We are judged in the most negative way without a fair evaluation. We seem to have this defamatory perception of us, people are repelled by just a glance. And despite the fact if we qualify for the job or not we're put through so many hurtles just to prove ourselves worthy to advance in any field of life.

Since the beginning of African people arrival to America in the earlier 1600s we've experienced so much hatred that it truly seems as if we developed that same hatred towards each other. As if we somehow became a product of the foul treatment and conditions that were forced upon us. These days it seems like a fashion or a trend with in our own communities to hate our own existence.

I wanted to address the issue again of there being a lack of unity in the black community. It's something that we aren't giving much attention to being that we are mainly focused on our own survival. The only time black people seem to share a bond of togetherness is when someone dies or too much injustice raised concerns.

When there's nothing to cry or complain about we see no means for being united. We're quick to turn on each other to prove there's no loyalty. We're quick to deny each other help to prove there's no favoritism. We are quick to condemn or criticize our brothers and sisters to prove we can also be hard on our own black people. We're quick to do everything that proves we are different from our own kind. Those who are still being affected by discrimination. Those who are struggling to excel in society because of the forces working against them. Those who would always be viewed the same no matter how much we try to relate to this society. You've only became another opposing opposition that they must worry about because of your means to prove you're not like us.

We have been afflicted with so much pain, so much grief, and so much adversity our entire lives. Not in the sense of it being individually but, generally black people haven't had it easy at all. There were many trials and tribulations we had to surmount. There were many obstacles and impediments we had to get through. There were many oppositions we had to face in the country. And we are still facing these oppositions today. I wanted to point out the oppositions we faced in the past till the ones we now face. Oppositions from slavery and the brutal acts back then till the same brutal acts now that continues to happen. Maybe not as much as then but some of the practices are still exercised.

This is another call to examine the person with in. To take a look at yourself. How could you hate yourself when your people have suffered enough already from the same evils your up against? The same evils that desires your hindrance, demise, or consider you nothing but a puppet in their grand scheme.

This is what I see when I view a reflection of my self-image. These are the thoughts conveyed by my conscious state.

The Black Fox

The black fox never howls at the moon,
Diffident that his wails wouldn't reach,

So, he retreats deep inside the peak of the mountain where he seeks refuge,

Discreetly distancing himself from the elite pack of wolves he feels he doesn't amount to,

Depressingly watching from a less discouraging location as his doglike predatory peers loudly yowl without fear,

Squealing and hollering through the night with a bravado of confidence that he unfortunately does not share,

Which causes him to resume in gloom,
Doubting that he could ever compare his groans to the moans they flare,

So, he stares in despair relinquishing his endeavors without care,

Stagnated by his defective ability that causes him to feel impaired,

So, he accepts defeat regretfully,
Knowing he'll never be content if he doesn't at lease try to persevere,

But he's more scared of failing then he's eager to succeed,

Pessimistic that he'll never be as gifted or possess such proficiency the other's received,

Because he suppresses his ambition beneath his indolent intentions to settle for something other then what he's destine to be,

Skeptic of the potential he fails to see,
Which cause a lack of diligence and a feeling of timidity,

Shutting himself out from the world because of this mental deficiency,

So, if you never hear the black fox howl at the moon again; Maybe he still hasn't yet found the confidence he needs to believe.

P.O.A.P

The Black Fox

THE BREAK DOWN

In this poem I wanted to convey the ideal of despair and having a sense of pessimism. I wanted to show the inertness we allow ourselves to be overcome with when we lose faith or confidence in our ability to prevail through inconceivable odd or obstacles. This poem is about the lack of motivation most people find themselves stagnated by. It's about being discouraged to pursue your goals because of self-doubt or a lack of conviction. Most people allow their desires to be restrained by temporary setbacks or defeat which can suppress their furtherance. Preventing them from advancing in their positions or status. Sometimes we allow hindrance to deplete us mentally and physically to the point we become lethargic in our efforts. Settling for a purposeless reality that doesn't require any determination or willfulness. A reality where people are impaired by the thought of failure. In the absence of motivation, we idly become content with laziness. And when we're dissuaded by discouragement our desires seem unobtainable. The Black Fox represents the gloomy state of despondency. It's not an interpretation of a particular person or group of people. It's a portrayal of any individual who doesn't feel as clever or crafty as his peers. It's about one who doesn't feel driven, skillful, creative, or capable enough to be as successful as other's. We all wish to be great achievers but often find ourselves pressured by expectations we are unsure we can amount to. Sometimes we fear not living up to a certain level of success. And sometimes that fear can cause us to abandon our endeavors and end up wallowing in our regrets or refusal to try.

The reason that "the Black Fox never howls at the moon" is because he lacks confidence that his wails would reach such a distance. This is a reference to the goals we set out to achieve that may seem unimaginable or like a façade. You see the wails isn't just the sound of a fox cries or complaints. It's the desperation and urgency that provokes us to procure the objectives we wish to attain. But sometimes that hope for prosperity seems unreachable and just makes us want to weep out of frustration. And when we feel that we don't have the will it takes to achieve our desires we desist in our pursuits thinking that the attempt isn't worth the struggle. But no hurtles can be measured without experience and every individual must account for their own observation of the trials life present them.

Sometimes when a person feels fruitless, he falls into a great depressive state of mind. He psychologically become dejected by his deficiency to create better conditions or possibilities for himself. And begin to carry a burden of misery. This burden causes dispiritedness and hopelessness. And often makes people feel embarrassed and ashamed of not being able to fulfill their wishes or show their brilliant potential. As a result, some people hide in an unconscious state when facing reality by not acknowledging their responsibilities. And others hide by closing themselves out from the world because that's the only time they'll feel safe and free from distress or being reminded of their relinquishments.

"So, when the black fox retreats deep inside the peak of the mountain where he seeks refuge", I'm talking about the person who shuts himself out from reality by becoming despondent." Discreetly distancing himself from the elite pack of wolves". The fox is one of the many flesh-eating mammals that are related to wolves. In actuality the fox is much smaller, has shorter legs, and a more pointed muzzle than the wolf who is much larger, has erected-ears, a bushy tail, lives and hunts in packs and is truly superior to the fox. But let's forget about the fact that a fox is known to be a quick and skillful predator. Remember this isn't an ordinary fox or a wolf we're talking about. We're just using a few comparisons in reference. This fox we're talking about is a lackadaisical fox that is immobilized by inefficiency. And the wolf we're speaking of is more sufficient and driven. I wanted to use the fox and the wolf as a metaphor to describe a person who has given up on himself, and a person who has excelled to a successful position. The relation of the fox and wolf shows that they are the same but different in appearance. Ambition and languor is also different in appearance. One has the eager desire to succeed which shows a diligent persistency to persevere, and the other is to be inactive which shows a torpid idleness. When a person achieves any kind of success they begin to feel elite in their confidence as if they can exceed at anything. They begin to give the impression that their more self-assured than ever. The wolf eats greedily at success while the fox looks forward to what he can easily gain without difficulty. The fox could never amount to the wolf because of its determination to thrive.

So, he "depressingly watch from a less discouraging location". The black fox would rather be anywhere else other than in an environment where he is always confronted by other's success or reminded of his failure and the fact that he hasn't yet reached a favorable outcome. To him it's almost like having their accomplishments rubbed in his face. Especially when "his doglike predatory peers loudly howling without fear". Fear of failing or experiencing temporary defeat themselves. Unlike the black fox they know the difference between failure and defeat. They know that failure is only a state of mind that is brought upon one self. They know how to pick themselves back up when they fall. They're persistent despite opposition or impediments that stands in the way of their progress unlike the black fox. But when the wolves "squeal and holler through the night with a bravado of confidence", it makes the black fox become frustrated and irritable to have to hear their boasting and bragging about what they've acquired. Because that is something "he unfortunately does not share".

That kind of situation can cause anybody to become dispirited. When you're a person who is already living with doubts about yourself or your ability, you tend to become a little more depressed at the thought of not being able to compare to others, not being able to share their attainments, or not being able to accomplish their goals. That would cause an individual to fall deeper into despair or feel like there's no need for them to keep trying if they'll never be as good as it takes. Because they're stagnated by the faultiness of not living up to normal standards or lacking in something necessary to be efficient. And having those kinds of thoughts can damage a person.

Even if you have people who allow their efforts to be subdue by defeat and accepts failure. Every day they are going to live with the regret of not at least giving it their best. They could never be content with surrendering to failure. They may fear failing more than they're eager to succeed, but they would never be satisfied with them self.

The black fox knows he'll never be as gifted as other's who bask in their success because he always takes the least favorable perception when seeing his own potential. He expects nothing but the worse results whenever he attempts to do something. That's "because he suppresses his ambition beneath his indolent intentions". Beneath the lazy exterior he displays, he restrains any thoughts of the urge to push himself or propel to action. And unlike the black fox, the wolf knows that success requires difficulty. He knows that obstacles are going to stand in its way, but he's aware that he must persist in order to prosper. The black fox on the other hand settles for a predetermined course of events where he refuses to see what's in his fate. "He's doubtful of the potential he fails to see". He doesn't feel he qualify or has the skills to carry out his vision, which diminishes his energy to be steadily active and cause a feeling of disbelief. And when a person has that kind of mentality it could shut them out from the world as much as they wish to hide from it.

"So, if you never hear the black fox howl at the moon again, maybe he still hasn't yet found the confidence he needs to believe", in himself, believe he can prevail over whatever hurtles, and believe he can achieve anything he put his mind to if he strives diligently enough to acquire it.

Choices

Let's talk about life and the decisions we make,

The choices and the options we choose from, but mistake that ache,

Painful regrets and culpable criticism we berate ourselves with; wishing we could change our fate,

Ignorant erroneous blunders done out of immaturity; thinking we have all the answers but inadvertently show up to the test late,

Failed miserably in our volition because of our imprudence and refusal to listen,

Sat back in the class being a distraction; causing a diversion for other minds in attendance,

Not knowing if this lesson was about our path; our purpose; or our mission,

The matter of whatever we decide is the result of how we end up living,

The matter that if we don't think wise; then the outcome would be the dumbest thing we felt we intended,

The matter that our neglect for the subject presented could cost us down the line if we're not attentive,

Because we chose to choose what we thought was right when we should have chosen to choose that which lost our interest,

You know that message the teachers of errors discussed while we continued to be inattentive,

Goofing off pretending to be the cool kids; obstinately repelled by any convincing.

So, we're taught an example which causes grief or affliction,

Misery or despondency; depending on the predicament we are in that distinguish our condition,

Forcing us to reflect on our comportment which earned us detention in any cogent position,

Transitory suspensions to make modifications so that our decorum is sufficient,

Or that we are not expelled permanently from the classes life presents us due to an unfortunate decision,

So, take heed When a lesson is giving,
And approach what's being taught with apprehension,

Because just maybe it could be a life changing volition that alters our existence,

Where an accurate and more vital selection is made; instead of going off intuition,

And end up wishing we could redo the errors committed; so that our choices turn out different.

Choices

THE BREAK DOWN

In the process of creating this poem I wanted to express the ideal of life reflecting a class room setting. I wanted to give the notion that shows a parallel comparison with both being a teacher of knowledge and experience. In life when we go through trials or adversity, we learn a great deal of things negatively and positively that help or derail us from our path. We learn how our choices affect other's or ourselves. We learn the outcome or results whether it's for the good of a cause or bad. We learn how to apply ourselves through efforts. And we learn from the mistakes we make after realizing our wrong. We learn many things just as in a class room. When in a class room we learn how to deal with multiple choices when figuring out an answer. We learn how to solve or calculate problems to the best of our knowledge. I wanted to show reader's how most of us treat life like being in school and are as negligent in our studies as those who don't really take their education serious. I wanted to show how they both, life and a class room, could be viewed the same when it comes to a person's future. In life you can't move forward without making the right decisions. Just as in school, you can't advance in your level of education without choosing the right decisions when your knowledge is tested. They both prepare us for our journey, missions, and experiments. But it's up to us to take heed from the lessons that are taught.

Let's talk about life and the importance of our volition. The choices and options we choose from that often dictate our future. It's just like being tested on a quiz. When we make the wrong decisions, they can sometimes hurt us. In a school setting, if we chose the wrong answers we are liable to get a low score, be held back to repeat our grade over, or would have to make up for it during a summer school program. Either way it can hurt us. It may not be as severe as the error's we make in life, but we are still affected by heedlessness.

In life the regrets are going to be more painful than the sorrow of missing out on summer fun or going through the same grade twice. But the rueful feeling of knowing you could have made better choices are always going to be the same. And we may scold ourselves harshly do to our negligence, because of the shame or humiliation of our inattentiveness which causes our furtherance to be suppressed temporarily. Without consciousness of our blunders, or us being mindless of our exams, even our own judgement of what we feel is right could go unnoticed. We must be culpable of our actions to realize what we need to do to improve our decisions.

Immaturity means lacking complete development. Not quite yet going through a natural process of growth, differentiation, or evolution. That natural process requires us to learn and retain knowledge that will assist us in our germination. Sometimes we must go through certain situations in order to know what to avoid and what not to. And sometimes it's obvious what we should embrace or stay away from. Sometimes as humans we think we have all the answers. And those answers are just assumptions often. There not definitely or exact. We sometimes refuse help because we feel like we could do things on our own. That kind of attitude is like preparing to take a test and being so confident that you are going to pass. You've studied so hard and diligent and just know you got all the answers. But still you show up late and fail because you forgot that the test starting time was an important requirement. It's never our attention to show up late after studying so hard. Most people show up ready and eager when they've studied determinedly. And you know those who studied so hard that they be sitting at the desk awaiting their test package and seem to just be bursting with narcissism. You can't tell them that they don't got this is the bag. And if you ask them they probably feel like they don't ever need any help. But they would realize that there are even better ways of coming to know things that would enhance their ability. That person in a class is sort of like the person in the street who feels that know one could tell them nothing. Like they got it all mapped out. We sometimes become too confident or arrogant that we feel we no longer need any help. But if we would just listen sometimes, we would receive the proper instructions we need to be on schedule that would broaden our creativity. We could have all the answer to everything in life and still not get it because we continue to fail miserable in our volition due to our lack of judgement and disregard for the advice that would provide our guidance with more clarity.

In school, you often have individuals who accept the cognomen of a class clown. They are the ones who sit back in the class room being a distraction to what's being taught. Their humor tends to deviate more than amuse. Their lack of interest to learn causes them to disrupt the other minds who are willing to retain any valuable information. In the real world you're going to have them same class clowns or bad influence who strive to distract your focus. They're the ones who has given up on their plans and wish to deter others in pursuit of their goals.

Sometimes we take the lessons we're presented for granted. We sometimes feel like we can afford to ignore certain examples because we don't think it's vital to our edification. So, we omit certain notes or skip out on classes that we feel isn't too important, not knowing or understanding how crucial they could have been to our life. Every lessons serves a purpose whether we believe it or not. When we're pursuing an education, we're given notes on everything we need that pertains to the subject in which we would be tested on. These notes are intended to assure that we are familiar with the topic's or exercises on our quiz. And that we get enough right answers to pass. In life, every lesson we're taught is significant as well. The experiences we go through prepares us for greater choices we may have to make. Choices that would be difficult to choose without being heedful to the lesson or mindful of the notes that was presented. The mental notes we make about our conduct and what we must do to better ourselves. Those are the notes that could determine how our lives would be affected by those greater choices. It's a matter of what we now decided could ultimately be an indefinite result. These notes we take in prevent us from having to guess or make the dumbest mistake we assumed to be assure of.

Our neglect for any subject could cost us. Whether it's now, tomorrow or later down the line. If were not attentive to the advice or enlightenment that's being offered, we could always end up losing. Because we may choose what we think, or feel is right, but instead chose what we were oblivious to because we didn't know.

The teachers of error's is a metaphor to describe those who were hindered by their blunders. Those who made too many wrong decisions in their lives and feel a need to admonish other's so that their life wouldn't be ruined by their poor choices as well. They are teacher's due to their instructive nature to educate people about the disagreeable consequences of an action. And also because of their cognizance which validate their degree of understanding. But we are often repelled by any convincing. We are so obstinately stubborn in our ways that we refuse to open up our minds to any lecturing. We rather goof off and play the cool kids like those individuals in school who seem to smooth to be taught anything, as if were too good for knowledge or a few suggestions on how we should live. When we neglect those suggestions, or the advice shared with us, we sometimes end up being taught a more severe lesson than we would rather. A lesson of affliction, grief, or despondency depending on the predicament that causes our condition. These lessons can force us to reflect on the choices we made out of foolishness. Our actions could constrain us to a period of detention to a hospital room, it could subject us to a brief suspension in our freedom and activities, in order to make amendments or adjustments to our behavior, or we can be expelled permanently by a fatal incident because of an unfortunate decision we made.

So, it's best we pay attention and show up to class prepared to take notice when we are being schooled by life's lessons. And approach what's being taught while viewing our future with anxiety. Because without the right guidance we could choose the worse volition that could alter the course of our lives. And being more attentive could help us make an exact or precise selection that's necessary for us to maintain, instead of just going off of what we assume we know. Just to end up wishing we could redo our error's if the opportunity still presents itself. Because in some cases we can't change our fate after the decision has been final.

IF the Truth Would Set You Free
What Would A Lie Do?

If the truth would set you free would a lie confine you to a reality that's govern by deceit?.

Is the truth reason for liberation while a lie tend to usually impede?,

Is the realization of the truth comforting while a lie makes other's feel unease,

If the truth would set you free would a lie encourage ones belief?,

Would the truth abolish whatever happiness while a lie incite felicity?,

Is the realization of the truth devastating or does a lie grants relief?,

If the truth would set you free would a lie spare the feelings of grief?,

Is the truth too cruel to receive while a lie provide thoughts of peace?,

Is the realization of the truth uncomfortable while a lie offers serene?,

If the truth would set you free would a lie suppress the misery?,

Is the truth the best solution or would a lie prevent hurt intentionally?,

Is the reality of the truth malicious while a lie provides sympathy?,

If the truth would set you free would you rather be given amnesty?,

Or would you prefer to lie to cover the shame and protect the feelings from treachery?,

Is the truth an honest necessity or is a lie despised regretfully?,

Because the realization is when the truth is stated a lie is sometimes favored exceptionally.

P.O.A.P

If the Truth Would Set Free
What Would A Lie Do?

THE BREAK DOWN

In this poem I wanted to question the notion of the truth versus a lie. I wanted to challenge the concept of what we believe is morally correct and the reality of what may be suitable for the preservation of one's condition, relationship, or beatification. It's human nature that we desire the truth more than anything. We crave the relief of incertitude and psychologically being free of any worries of mistrust. We hate to be deceived so much that in most cases a lie tends to become the main focus in the offense rather than the action which sometimes is no longer the main issue. We hold a lie to be more severe or damaging then any betrayed act because of the dishonesty and reliance that was breached. The trust that grants an assurance of tranquility and dependency. When a lie is told it makes us view people differently. It makes us doubtful of their intentions or devotion. But is the truth always good? Is the truth really what we wish to hear in most cases? And once hearing the truth would it cause more damage than a lie? Because if the truth would set the person who admits their wrong free, what would a lie do?

If the truth was to set a person free, would telling a lie then confine one to deceitful measures? Would one feel govern by the verity that's concealed to manage that lie? We know once a person tells a lie they end up being bounded by that lie. They'll have to follow up with a whole bunch of others lies until they are caught up in a web full of fabrication. Most people are compulsive liars and can't help but to feed their habit to delude other's. And some people are just afraid of the extent the punishment may carry when exposing the truth. Other's claim to have lied to protect one's emotions from being hurt. But regardless of any circumstances do we think that a lie is mostly required? Do we believe it's harmful or shielding?

It's a question of opinions but to be considered with logical determination. Is the realization of the truth comforting? Do we really rather hear the truth when it's demanded? Does this truth grant a piece of mind or freedom from grief? Does it provide uneasiness. Or does a lie offer more than the feeling of disappointment or anger? Does it bestow solace? Do a lie impede the feelings or is the truth more devastating. Because if the truth is meant to set a person free from having to keep in a lie, the guilt of hurting someone feelings can prevent the admission of the truth by choosing to lie.

Would a lie encourage one's belief? Would it further the tenacity to be diligent in their commitment? Would it strengthen the faith in those we feel we can rely on or to be trustworthy? Or would the truth destroy their unwavering attachment? Sometimes the truth does more harm than a lie. It often abolishes one's felicity rather than retain it or maintain its current state. And a lie, although it's frowned upon, causes the feelings to feel secured and safe. I'm not saying it's cool to lie even if the intentions are good. I'm just asking how many of us think hearing the truth is always better for us?

We must look at who's receiving this freedom by telling or hearing this truth. Is it the one who is admitting their wrong or is it the one who just wish to know the honest account. Because if the accused is being freed then we must assume that the accuser is being burdened. So, would a lie actually spare the feelings from having to bare the misery of hearing this distressing news? The truth is sometimes cruel and inconsiderate. It doesn't have any regard for the feelings of other's. It doesn't sympathize with the pain of being let down. But could a lie empathize with the stress or aggravation that one becomes depressed about? Not knowing the truth of something that is extremely afflicting or devastating, is more exonerating for both parties, rather than facing the painful fact that is damaging to both. So, is the realization of knowing the truth uncomfortable or does a lie offers one serenity?

Would the truth honestly be the best solution, or would a lie save others from a disastrous gloom? The truth is honest and exact. It's apparently blunt and cuts no corner. Sometimes it could seem malicious because of the offense that we testify to. Sometimes people are more distressed by the truth then a lie. But the falsehood one swears by can leave more of a heartless impression. When we are lied to, we feel as though we aren't loved. We feel like we don't matter enough to be told the truth. Our feelings don't seem to be acknowledged or any concerns to those who lie during our quest for the truth. Although our feelings weren't considered in the initial violation technically. It could be assumed that no matter if the truth is heard or a lie is given, people's feelings are still going to get hurt. But that's not what we're talking about here, I want to know is telling a lie more of a horrifying tale then the truth? And does the truth makes people more bitter once it's revealed? A true admission frees only the guilty. So, does that make a person selfish to bound another to agony? Because though a lie can cause disappointment it could also protect a person from the true nature of things.

We know that lying doesn't better any situation. Especially when we keep having to make up excuses for what we do and why we did it. The truth can be forgiven within time just as well as a lie would. But the trust would never be broken when telling the truth versus a lie. You'll have to earn back the honor of reliance after being forgiven when you lie. It's necessary to have hope in the people we rely on because without it we could never be confident that they could ever have our best interest. And a lie makes it hard to believe in someone like that. So, whether we lie to cover up the shame or to protect the feelings from feeling betrayed, we still end up causing people anguish in the end. A lie can be painfully regretted but at the same time favored exceptionally because of the effect it has when the truth isn't discovered. But telling the truth prevents the greater damage which can ruin relationships because of the mistrust.

Juelz

A jewel that is hidden where the eyes could never see,

A diamond that continues to shine even when knowledge isn't received,

Because the greatest treasure don't grant wisdom to the poorest mind with fancy dreams,

And you're a rare quality that a jeweler has never seen,

And a buyer has never glanced upon because your worth seem too extreme,

People may question your beauty because your worth can't be obtain,

And most may even treat you cruelly but when you hurt it cause me pain,

And they don't understand beyond reason; because their actions have no shame,

And I don't understand their reason so I go off what I think,

And just to make sure your not grieving I'm protective of everything,

But it's impossible to believe and still claim to be a saint,

God's gift wouldn't you think,
Perfectly far from being flawed,

Makes perfect sense since God intent was to make us all the way he thought,

An autistic gem they can't afford,
From an artistic sense; that can't be bought,

A mother glitz,
A donor quits,
Which to me is hard to be ignored,

And just to vent I'm not convinced,
I'm trying to get how could a parent deny such a bliss,

I mean if; I was provided the privilege I would make it my business to make sure you never felt fatherless,

Or different in any case because truthfully no one actually knows what normal is,

And what I see is normal kid that they normally misunderstand,

But that goes to show that normally most people fail to comprehend,

And I promise to be the man who's there to make them understand,

And show them that true bling is like exchanging wedding bands,

A jewel you are Juelz; And your value has no cost,

You'll never feel forsaken by deception that's immature,

Or neglected by selfish acts that forget to show their support,

I just wish to be the dad to teach you what I wasn't taught,

Who cares to guide you through life course when your path isn't clear to walk,

And what's assumed as prison talk came out greater then what they thought,

That's predictions in advance of a future already sort,

A jewel that's seen and causes awe,
But Juelz to me your so much more,

The son I envisioned in a dream and an obligation I can't abort,

You'll always be my Juelz forever no matter the price it cost,

Forever Juelz.

P.O.A.P

Juelz

THE BREAK DOWN

This poem is more intimate to me than any of the other poems I've written. Although every poem I have conveyed in this book has been inspired by a personal affect or encouraging motivation that has influenced me in some way, this was truly a private and touchy matter that was triggered more so by a personal connection that binds me to a child as his father, and the feeling of wanting to provide him with the best care and support. It's about the love and devotion I intend to provide him with. And my vow to be a consistent part of his life. It's about a man who understands this young boy's need of male's guidance and the commitment he has made to take on the responsibility as his father. The responsibility that was left behind, which prevents him from feeling desolated because of his condition or the neglect that was displayed by the absent figure who walked out of his life. The responsibility of being a present factor and assisting in every moment of growth that leads to this young boy coming into a man. The responsibility of equipping him with the understanding, guidance, and monition that is vital. It's about a father who is aware of his child emotions. And the effect abandonment would mentally have on him. It's the acknowledgement of a man who is conscious of a child's true worth and importance and is committed to making sure that his value is always known. I wanted to dedicate a poem to my son that would show my sincere obligation and promise to be the father that has never neglected him, deserted him, or deprived him of love. Something that he would grow to understand in the future but acknowledge through my present actions, that would validate this pledge of mines. And contribute something special to him that would assure him of how much he means to me. And although Juelz which is my son's name, would technically be considered as my step son being that I didn't assist in his conception, I wanted to make sure that my acknowledgement of him actually being viewed as my biological son is the only way I'll ever perceive him, and that I would genuinely treat him as such regardless of what can be proved otherwise.

I wanted to point out his condition of autism which is a social disorder that is characterized by the impaired ability to communicate with others and form normal social relationships, that most people fail to recognize being that they do not know him or his circumstances. But I wanted to make it known that despite his condition I would do my best to make sure that he never felt impaired nor disabled in any way by this disorder. This poem is about my oath to stand by his side and be there to protect him from the harsh views of a world that may judge him wrongly because of his condition. And show him that he's just as capable, qualified, or entitled to anything in life as anyone one else. It's a reminder that he is never alone and will always have a true dad in his life to provided him with the best care he could ever be afforded.

We all know that the most precious thing is a life form or the birth of a child. There is nothing more incredible or greater than the existence of a human being. We are the most extraordinary creation this world has ever possessed. I wanted to make the comparison of the most precious gift that could be given to a woman out of affection. A gift other than a child which is jewelry or diamonds. It's a known fact that women love jewelry, and nothing brings them more satisfaction then having a brilliant mineral that sparkles. Though costly or not it confirms the validation of love that a male has for a woman. And out of affection it's provided majority of the time. A child could be looked at or viewed in the same manner being that it's out of affection that we plan or unplanned to conceive. Because of our affectionate desires we sexually engage in activities that sometimes result in the birth of a child, although the commitment to adhere to a responsibility isn't always fulfilled. I also wanted to show the significance behind the name Juelz and what it means. Juelz as in "jewels" being a diamond in the rough, which represents his worth despite his condition. And I wanted him to come to know that a man's oath defines the character he conceals and reveals the true intentions behind his words.

I had decided to start this poem off with the metaphor of knowledge being presented. It's a term we often use when someone delivers enlightening or meaningful advice which is called "dropping jewels" as a reference of dropping knowledge. It's the only jewel that the eyes could never see no matter what. Even though diamonds are buried beneath whatever lands or hidden from sight. It's possible that they still can be found with persistent search methods. But knowledge that's receive isn't found by sight it's only obtains by consciousness. But I also wanted to make known that we're still talking about an actual diamond in the second line of the poem. Although knowledge can be hidden from sight it doesn't continue to shine as a diamond would if it's not being applied. A diamond may become clouded and dull a bit, but it never loses its shine. And in this poem the thing that's meant to represent the diamond's (which is Juelz) "shine", is the acknowledgement of his existence and the responsibility that one should always be conscious of.

Now we all know that the greatest treasure does not provide wisdom. Nor does the smallest. But most people think that money could solve problems, which it doesn't. The wealthiest person could still be the poorest mentally. And make the most foolish choices that would cost them their fortune. By this I am referring to the value of a child which is the greatest treasure one could ever procure and the poor decision of negligence a parent display. Having a child doesn't qualify a person to be a parent. It doesn't grant them good judgement or make them knowledgeable in this area. Though their course of actions should be more wiser.

Now the mention of a rare quality and jeweler is another metaphor. It's speaking of a rare quality which is birth of a child. That's something an actual jeweler has never seen in a jewelry shop unless someone had given birth right there in the store, which would still be something that is rare. But it is also a reference to the quality of a diamond. A diamond that is so unique and so unusual that a jeweler has never set his eyes on it or seen the like of. And a buyer has never even looked at it or in its direction, if it was available because the worth would be so extreme that they probably couldn't ever buy it. By this I also mean the "buyer" being the men who sees the obligation of being with a woman with a responsibility as a burden. The worth of this realization to them seems too extreme.

And the people that question your beauty are those who doubt the quality of that diamond being that it may have a great shine to it or is prominent in seize. Because of its difference from the normal diamonds they see makes them question its value. This is kind of like a kid with a conditional problem that they question his ability to function like a normal kid. So, they rather disassociate themselves rather then deal with his disorder. For example, there was a problem that happened at my child's school that was very disturbing and upsetting. I admit it he was wrongfully biting and spitting at the teacher. So, they had insisted that my wife put him on medication rather than considering other solutions or methods that would be less numbing or sedating. I was truly angered more by their suggestions then my son's actions being that they are teacher's inside an educational system that should be founded on the development of the psychological functioning of our children being that these teachers are the ones who are training them to think by what they teach them. Of course, it's the duty of the parent to institutionalize the best mannerism. But these kids are spending a significant amount of time at school as well, for them not to learn proper propriety. And it's the last thing any human being should be suggesting for a kid anyhow. Because of his condition they felt that was the best alternative, and that was only the first time that had happened. To me that was the cruelest thing that occurred during that entire incident. And I only imagine my son being aware of what was going on. I thought about him having sound understanding to comprehend the situation and how much hurt that probably would have caused him. And it was me considering his feeling when I had advised my wife what should be considered and how I felt about his teachers and school. I told her a bunch of things that I can't remember and wouldn't wish to repeat that were negative about those teachers and their system that governs them. It was his hurt that caused me pain.

And for one to recommend medication for a 6-year-old they can't truly understand beyond reason that something like that is the evilest thing. Especially when their actions have no shame, as if what they do or say is appropriate. And that's something I don't understand so I could only make it my intentions to protect my child under any circumstances. And by any means if necessary which is a general statement.

Every religion acknowledges the fact that God made Adam with his bare hands. Unlike every other creation we were given his effortless labor. An effort that didn't require much to a God but an effort that was made. It's said that angel's and Jinn's which is the devil was a word that came forth. We are the most perfect thing because of this. We are his perfection with defects, flaws, conditions and all. But it's no reason to explain that if people don't see the beauty in every one of God's creations, just as the books God sent forth can't be explained to a person who don't believe. And how could those who do claim to be a saint say that they believe if they don't acknowledge a person with blemishes as more of special addition to life. We are all God's gift so even with flaws we are still perfect. How could we not be when it was God's intent to make us all the way he thought. And what could ever be more perfect then God's thoughts.

I wanted to show a genius comparison between my son, his condition, and the relation to a jewel. So, I thought that an autistic gem was the most perfect figure of speech that would represent him. Because a gem is a jewel, but it's also something that is valued for its beauty or perfection. So, his condition doesn't take away from his beauty or perfection, it adds to it making him more special. And that's something no one can't afford to ignore, because to love a child is to love them unconditional. And from an artistic sense, that means viewing them just as perfect as you would without any debilities. And nothing shows more love then the bond that binds a father to his child which could never be sold. It must be earned through the quality time that familiarize that kinship.

When it comes to jewelry or diamonds, woman seem to be the most fascinated by its decor and expensive glamour then anyone. It's marvelous designs and contrasting styles are a sore eye for women's taste and gives a variety of precious adornments that suits their desire. To women jewelry makes them feel powerful. Back in the late 2000's b.c. Egyptians believed that gems had magical powers and wore them for good luck. But truly the ability to give birth to a human life is more powerful than any jewelry could ever make a woman feel. And luck is the capability to succeed through chance or good fortune which is the unpredictability or sufficiency of raising a child with or without a companion. But the glitz of a child is the only jewelry that a woman will ever truly adore with all her heart.

Most people assume the role of a father even when there not present in their child's life. They claim to be a dad when they never adhered to the responsibilities that entitles them to accept such acknowledgement. Fatherhood requires more than the provision of sperm fluids. It requires more than genetic contributions. Women who wish to be impregnated without the hassle of having to deal with no good men, tend to seek options of being fertilized with sperm provided by donors at hospital fertilities. It's a shame that men participate in these arrangements or that women even consider having a child without knowing the identity of the father because it takes away from that kid being raised by a male without choice. But the only difference between the donor that supplies the hospitals with sperm and a person who abandons a child is that the confidentiality is known. Which only makes it more shameful that one would neglect their child or deny them their right to have a father. But to vent, I want to know how could any parent deny such a bliss? How could one desert such a joy? If I had the chance I would make sure that any child I have the opportunity of raising, never feels fatherless. Or different in Juelz case because know one really knows what normal is. Meaning that we all have special and unique abilities that sets us apart from one another. So how could we be normal when we are so different from one another? If we were thought to be normal wouldn't we all be the same? So, under those circumstances all I see is a normal kid who is misunderstood. But that's just because normally most people have a failure to comprehend the things they can't figure out. But as a father, it's my duty to help them understand even if I must make them. And show them that true bling is like exchanging wedding bands. Now this was a reference to the proposal I made to his mom, my wife. And the promise of me being his father till death do us part. It's the only true "bling" or jewelry that could ever be considered as sincere because of the oath that is mentioned before exchanging rings. Anything else doesn't come with such a vow so it isn't true. And this also could be taken as the distinction between a mature man and one who hasn't grown to understand the responsibility of marriage or having a child. To most men bling is regular jewelry that doesn't come with a contract of commitment.

I wanted my son Juelz to know that he is a jewel and his value has no cost. He doesn't come with a price or a return warranty. His value is far greater than any jewelry that can be purchased though the obligation of being the father figure in his life is not for sale.

I just wanted to let him know that this promise I made was more than just me giving my word to be there. Most kids are unfamiliar with the men that come in and out of their mother's lives. Their only aware of their presence but doesn't really know the circumstance being their too young to understand fully or aren't informed on the details of the situation due to it being the business of adults. But I wanted these words to be my testimony, my contract of agreement to what I had promised. I wanted him to know that he would never be forsaken by deception that's immature. Meaning that he wouldn't be abandoned because of false intentions or unctuous talk just to win his mon's affection, forgetting to consider the welfare of feelings of a child who could also be affected by a man's mendacious intention. Nor would he ever be neglected by selfish acts that forget to show their support. "Selfish acts" which are the selfish desire that are pursued with the performance of gaining an interest that is only benefiting to the individual themselves and no other party. It's the act that forgets to show its support because of their selfish neglect.

And although this poem is about me being a father to a child. It's also about me having a son to love as my own. A son I can show the love I never received from my "donor" or sperm provider. It's about me and this child having something in common with desertion and me seeing myself in this child. And realizing how important it is for that void of dereliction to be filled. How important it is to be provided the right advice and have someone genuinely there who is concerned about the path you're going to take in life. And I just wish to be that dad to teach him what I wasn't taught by my dad because of his failure to be involved in the process of my growth. A dad who cares to guide him through difficult, hardship, or conflicting predicaments that makes his progression hard to achieve.

The thing about people finding love with individuals who are incarcerated is that everyone seems to be against it. Family, friends, and even associates. No one thinks that women and men are capable of building a veracious, prosperous and salubrious relationship from an unfavorable and condemning place. Either because they assume that a person who has made an error couldn't be trusted or because they feel that a felon can't offer nothing but stress and depression. But what's not realized is that you can't claim to hate a thing or be disgusted by it and still accept to love the same thing because you choose to view it different. Meaning that there are many people who make mistakes. There are many people who were felons that people accept without judgement. Like Martha Stewart for example. She went to jail for a violation of the law, but America still loves her. And I for one view her with a high regard. But I'm just making a point that, what can be assumed as "prison talk" or for a more broad understanding "false promises from prisoners of desperation", by those who do not wish to see two people happy because of the terms of their relation would be proven by me, as far as my promise to be greater then what they thought when I'm released. And that's a prediction in advance of a future I'm already investing in. A future I'm already bringing to realization by every intention I put forth. I've took it upon myself to make my wife apart of everything I'm invested in to show her that my dreams and plans for the future involves her and my son and this is not just a reach for companionship to get me through difficult times.

Sometimes when jewelry is being worn, especially in a public outings it causes people to take notice. It causes them to stop and stare because of its sparkle or glitter. It causes them to direct their attention to the flashy item they see because it has captured their interest. But with this particular jewelry representing a child the attention it demands means so much more. He's more than just a sight for attraction. He's more than just a showy extravagant item to accessorize ones look. He's like a mirror image of myself because of the hand he was dealt and the reality that awaits him. He's also everything I ever imagined my son would be. And the responsibility I told myself I would never abort if presented the opportunity to prove what a father should be to his child. He's my "Juelz forever" as a referral to the saying diamonds are forever no matter the price it cost, in which I'm talking about the effort, energy, or strength it takes to raise him into a man. And to me he'll forever be recognized as a jewel.

Ghetto love the Broadway musical

When the rhythm flow caught up in the madness; Got me asking where and how did I stumble upon such passion,

True love,

Where the men don't really do love; Because the trust been breached so many times that they find themselves saying screw love,

But crew love make them seem real; Where schemes kill and lock them up leaving bastard's,

Now that's cruel ain't it? But that's usually how it happens,

And that's the way it's painted in the galleries of the ghettos tragic,

Far from Picasso's though their bravado show exhibits of ignorant colossal that depict their own debacles,

Now that's some artwork ain't it?

Where the brush stroke leads to death row; And there's dead folks who use to be their peers,

Now they share more hatred then their leggo's; And dying for a cause which seems more fulfilling then the comfort of a woman even if they don't claim so,

But that's love there; And this isn't considered love here,

But honestly; it's love here that changes thugs here,

But these type of feelings to another villain a get you plugged here,

And them thugs there; They usually shed blood there,

But this is more then us being a rug here with a coffin beneath and those who was here,

I'm just admitting what scares most to love them doves here,

I'm talking educated women bright and beautiful,

The type that's dutiful and make life more suitable; and your plights more doable,

And has potential to become that wife who makes you want to do right and be that knight that she views in you,

But they addicted to a life that would ruin you,

So, what if…So what if I see better; That make me soft cause I'm not choosing you,

And rather choose a woman who's love causes way less funeral's when the commitment is equally mutual,

And the intentions isn't disguised behind deceit where the lies aren't renewable,

This is genuinely sincere,
And this is to memories we'll share,

This is ghetto love the Broadway musical.

P.O.A.P

Ghetto Love the Broadway Musical

THE BREAK DOWN

In this poem I wanted to show the two kinds of love that men in the street acknowledge besides the affection from family. One love which is from a woman, that is often disregarded and referred to as weak. And the love received from affiliates of a crew which is viewed as real. Most men in the streets grow up thinking that it's manly or macho to recognize the latter more so then the first. As if their too ashamed to have any kind of sensitive feelings. I wanted to show the difference between these two kinds of love which can either be harmful or good. The love that has been a hindrance and the love that has been inspiring. When in the streets the intentions could be assumed to be good as well. But only to further the wrong cause. We don't believe that our reality isn't true or the correct way to live because of all the distractions that keeps us unaware. And in that reality sentimentality doesn't have a place. Because only the strong survive in the arena of barbarians and those that show compassion are vulnerable to death much quicker, at least that's how things are perceived. But they do not realize that the love of a woman is more pleasant and stress free from all the conflicting things that severely agonize them. It's more comforting and soothing. It's also warm and concerning. It's gentle and easy when a man is sure of what he wants and the significance of what he has. And it's genuine when the commitment is veracious. A lot of men believe that loving a woman makes them a sucker but, loving their crew makes them tough. When you compare the two, having love for the crew is more damaging and destructive then providing love to a female. So, you'd be a sucker to desire something unwholesome rather then something that is healthy. But it's not thought

53

which is more noxious than the other. And though my objective is to show that loving a woman is more salubrious then having love for your crew I don't want readers to think that I'm excoriating the ideal of crew love or what it represents. I'm just trying to give a better perception of the way we view our women when it comes to love.

Now in this poem I chose to start off with "when the rhythm flow", because there's always a frequency or a grove that I channel into which stirs the course of my thoughts. It's almost like a madness overcomes me that is more genius then insane. A madness that allows me to articulate concepts that are apparent but eludes the mind so often. Concepts of realism that we don't actually ponder on though it's a normalcy. And in this madness, I was wondering where and how did I stumble upon such passion. Now this could be viewed in two ways. The passion as in my love for a woman or, the object of enthusiasm when it comes to my poetic expressions. It's a witty way to comprise both as a reference, while giving the assumption of one. I honestly had two perspectives in mind when I thought about love. I had my beautiful partner and soul mate in mind as well as my desire for success. More so my wife actually just to avoid being in the dog house. So, when it's thought that this poem is only speaking of a woman, the obvious becomes transparent only after the advisement of this break down that the passion of my talent is also what I'm referring to.

True love is something that isn't always obtained. Some people find love, but it isn't true. It's mostly considered blind love because of the false perception it gives. True love is sincere and free from devastation. It has disappointments but not in a treacherous way. I wanted it to be known that what I'm speaking of is genuine and absolute. The love shared that's full of pure intentions. And this love could be from a woman or it could be from whatever passion that drives you to success.

This love I'm referring to isn't something that the miscreant men do. It's not pursued by those who are criminal or possess a deviant mind frame. Because it's a righteous love. A love that is sensitive due to the nature of circumstances. It's not the kind of feelings thugs are comfortable with sharing because of their doubts of meeting an honest woman or being successful in a positive way. And the trust that has been breach is the efforts that has been rejected or denied. It's the impediments that keep suppressing one's furtherance to progress or it could be regarded as the women who aren't loyal or trustworthy. The scandalous type who is amorously insatiable.

Now when it comes to crew love. Most men in the streets vow a secret oath of fealty to the comrades they hang with. And this discreet pledge prohibits anything that contradicts its affiliation. Meaning that failure and success doesn't coincide. Just as a woman who wish for her companion to change his behavior, doesn't coincide with him living corrupt. This junction only welcomes iniquitous reinforcement where the schemes leads to death or jail, and cause families to become divided or children to grow up without no dads which is a cold reality. But it's the truth we usually see.

The ghetto is like an art gallery. It has many paintings which represent the lives that exist there. Paintings of the suffering, joy, and pain. But this depiction that is being viewed is one of the pictures of tragic. The tragic of these men brought on by their own disasters because of their ignorant conduct. They are devoted to their own abolition because they chose to take a route that doesn't requires earnest determination or commitment. But even this is the most brilliant display of portraits because art imitates life. But in this sequence, life is projecting the art I'm conveying to show the senseless actions these men are dedicated to. Which is the truest artwork one will ever be able to illustrate. Where the brush stroke of this tragic reality could lead to death row. And the dead folks are the lost souls caught up by the streets. Those who thought a life of crime was more promising. And most of the people who became the victims of ignorance that was once familiar with their offenders. They could have been buddies or just known acquaintances, but the streets made them enemies who now shared more hate for each other than the toys they once lent to one another, which shows their closeness. It's crazy that these outlaws would rather die for a cause that's vain then to give their life to a better purpose or settle for the comfort of a woman that isn't that sever. But to them, there's no love better than that which they are sacrificing their lives for.

The righteous pursuit for success isn't the kind of love the men in the streets favor being that the hustle game is more pleasurable. Just as the love for a woman isn't viewed as fondly because it takes away from that satisfaction also. Any love apart from the streets with those who aren't associated isn't fancied due to the possibility or affect it may have to change a person's heart from the wrong path. And when your married to the game infidelity isn't acceptable just as any true marriage. So, most are considered to be traitors when pursuing success or a woman, to a person who is involved in the streets because, the heart can truly only be reserved for the affection of one or the other. And the streets are the most selfish lover there could ever be, and sharing isn't something it would ever consider. But we all know the saying, to most "ignorance is bliss" so most men are content with being in error.

But if these thugs or street individuals would take the time to open up their minds, they would realize it's actually love here that would change them for the better. A love that would make them more fruitful and prosperous then they could have imagined, if only they'll make an effort to do something more constructive or achieve something more effective. By this love, I'm meaning a positive way of thinking that is more healthy, safe, and thoughtful of their wellbeing. It's more magnifying and progressive. And doesn't plan to use them till it's no longer a necessity. "but in order to receive this good wholesome love, they have to be willing to come out of that baneful mentality. They must be willing to open up their hearts to a love that's more pure and leave the streets alone period because, these kind of feelings of change or gentle affection may come off to another thug who has no conscience, as a vulnerable opportunity to attack being that one is now becoming aware of his self-value. And when your apart of them streets, you know that having a moral outlook can be a liability.

But this poem is more than us as a people being laid to rest like a rug or buried beneath dirt. Buried with the people who had died because of the same mentality. Those who use to be here that are glorified idly. It's about doing the right thing or loving the right woman. It's about what scares most men to strive for the good they desire. And I'm just admitting what scares them to love them doves. Almost like I'm an advocate of peace for the peaceful policy that will better their chances.

I wanted to give the impression of a dove to also represent the characteristics of a woman who is bright, successful, beautiful, and has integrity. One who is trustworthy and devoted. Doves are birds that can be defined as any numerous of pigeons. And the word pigeon is also used as a terminology to describe a particular type of woman. A woman of low quality, class, or morals. A woman that can't be trusted or is always a disappointment. Though I believe a pigeon is a poor choice of comparison when judging any woman, I just wanted to use an example that could be easily understood to those in the streets without being too complex. And show the difference between the two types of women that can be confused being that they are of the same kind with different standards of morals. One being a dove which represents something much more peaceful and noble, and one being a pigeon which represents something foul and obscene.

When I talk about being dutiful I'm referring to the conduct and actions that are validated by one's commitment to an occupation or position. The occupations which we legitimately pursued that are conducive to our growth or the position of a dutiful woman that deserves our tenacious devotion. I'm speaking of striving for something virtuous and ethical. Living a conformable life style that doesn't involves risk or chances nor is a danger to your wellbeing. It's the passion to succeed that a person would cherish without jeopardizing their life. Or having the position of a woman who is dedicated and obedient to the articles of union. One who is eager to fulfill her required task of cultism and take care of her obligations as your companion. A woman who makes life more suitable and easier. And your plights more enduring or capable of being managed. That special person who just make you want to do right and live appropriate to customs. A woman who views you as the knight she always envisioned for herself.

Not the position of those who wish to place you in endangering predicaments or calamities. Or wish to subdue your honest advancements or achievements. But it's a shame that most would rather be in a position that is impeding then to ascend. Their more loyal to a cause that has been a depressingly devastating epidemic. They rather commit to an occupation that only fulfills tragedy or punishment. It's like their addicted to a life that would ruin them completely instead of granting them sure prosperity without resulting in the demise of their existence.

When it comes to changing our characteristic's or habits, it isn't always an easy transition or something that most people can accomplish. When we set out to modify some of the things that are dissatisfying or disapproving which pertain to our attitude or actions, we encounter oppositions that are a hindrance to us making those proper adjustments. Oppositions that rather us remain in the same barren state. When most men in the streets see another person trying to do good or improve them self, they begin to ridicule or criticize that person efforts or abilities to amend his comportment. They wish to deter his plans of refinement because they refuse to accept change their self. So, they intend to discourage them by belittlement or disparaging names such as "sell out, scared straight, or sucker for love" when that love isn't devoted to their cause. If a person chooses a better way or kinder love they consider them soft because they no longer prefer the anguish of their prior engagements. And they rather choose a life that causes way less funerals or grief when the feeling is equally mutual. When it comes to success the desire for one to achieve is the only intended motive being that one would only obtain success once you have succeeded at accomplishing your pursuits. And when it comes to the streets it has no lucid intentions. It's caught in between failure and success. Although, it's more in accord with failure because of the illegitimate things that are indulged in. But in the streets when you fail it often leads to injury, death, or incarceration.

And when the commitment of a woman is equally mutual is doesn't involve funeral's neither. We know that some women are the cause to many conflicts. Some women were the reason for bad blood between men and countries as well as for most wars that were started. That's because their commitment wasn't reciprocal. They weren't loyal to the companion they professed to love. Their intentions were disguised behind deceit. When the love is equally mutual you wouldn't have to worry about treachery or distrust. You wouldn't have to worry about defending your honor because of the breach of commitment displayed by your spouse. You wouldn't have to worry about killing for or dying over someone who never was yours. And this is genuinely sincere enlightenment that I hope would better our pursuit for finding a healthier love.

This poem is dedicated to the memories that will be shared when you do embrace a better life for yourself. This is the breakdown of ghetto love the Broadway musical.

Judged as a Jezebel

It's a question of conformity and the propriety of what's considered to be improperly,

What's condemnatory but not sinisterly like the queen and her apostasy,

It's more about the sexual urges that define our women and the scrutiny because of hypocrisy,

I'm speaking of the jezebel's; the desirable unchaste jezebel,

A scope where opinions doesn't serve any merit but it's usually a democracy,

The liberation of free spirits having volition and no sexual limits while practicing monogamy,

And promiscuous women who loves that comfort of a warm body,

Jezebel; oh, could it be so my jezebel,

It's the confusion of prostitutes and committed women who simply wish to experience lustful curiosities,

So, your given the impression your imprudent transgression is lewd according to other's philosophies,

Ridiculed for what you do with whom you pursue mutually in privacy,

Jezebel for whom are thou jezebel,

Condemned for your suggestive expressions since your expected to present yourself modestly,

Stereotyped for your intemperance by society because of your sultry sexuality,

Thought to be scandalous although you conduct yourself with morality,

Oh, jezebel why be disparaged as thou jezebel,

And even though it's known you're a freak in the bedroom; Doesn't mean you owe anyone an apology,

Criticized for being unrestrained or unreserved whether it's with multiple partners or the one companion you claim,

Insulted with names that are intended to equate you with misconceptions which are offensive that makes you feel demeaned,

Jezebel why be hard on thou jezebel,

Such as "loose, fast tailed, hoe" or even a thot so that you believe your actions are obscene,

Judged by sexist and conservative respective's who rather your sexiness be constrained,

And your urges or desires of titillating satisfaction continue to be tamed,

Jezebel how did you come to be thou Jezebel,

Psychologically forcing you to think that your comportment is taint or isn't in accordance with proper decorum,

In order to convince you to refrain from exploring sexual heights and settle for a sex life of reformed boredom,

Due to what they view should cause shame,
Cause your desires to be hidden and disregarded as taboo or strange,

Jezebel where have you gone my beautiful jezebel,

Resorting to customary performance since you deem to be a jezebel being that your inhibition lacks restriction that should be bounded by what other's think,

Or because your wanton lasciviousness is too explicit,

As if what you do with your personal life should make other's feel offended,

My jezebel it's no one's business my sweet jezebel,

But how ever you choose to live is your discretion no matter whoever opinion makes you feel threatened,

As long as you can live happily with the choices you make; pay no attention to what they mention nor the misjudgment of their perception.

My jezebel my beautiful beloved jezebel.

P.O.A.P

Judged as a Jezebel

THE BREAK DOWN

It's unfair how much women are underestimated or devalued. How they're viewed more for their sexual explicitness then their miraculous achievements. I wanted to contribute something to the women who are judged because of their personal discretions and criticize for prudent indulgence that triggers misconceptions. The women who has offered more to be viewed then their sexual participation. I wanted to dedicate something that lets them know their sexual inhibition isn't no one's concerns. And that they shouldn't makes excuses or feel ashamed because of what others perceive them as. Throughout history women have been viewed insignificantly or has usually had fewer rights and a lower social status then men. They had traditional roles such as a wife or a stay at home mom that were expected of them. Women has always been held to an inferior standard compared to men and hardly recognized for their intellect or creativity. Many sociologists and anthropologist maintain that various cultures have taught women to behave accordingly to negative stereotypes. Stereotypes that keeps them restricted to a certain exceptional way of living. Women have fought for equal rights and acknowledgement for years. But society had fallen short on providing them their full accreditation throughout time. And still tarnish their accomplishments by pointing out their lewd intimacies to make them seem obscene or ill-suited to be praiseworthy.

This poem is to abolish the misjudgment of women due to their sexuality. It's a question of compliance and what is socially acceptable in conduct and speech according to the standards set by men. The standards that only apply to women, governing the way they should act or present themselves outside as well as inside their homes. As if their personal affairs should be viewed in decorum by society.

It's what has been declared unfit or wrong but, not productive of evil like the queen of Israel who name was Jezebel, The wife of Ahab in the bible. The woman who is noted for her malicious intent to lead people astray in their worship. I wanted to make known that it's not that kind of Jezebel we're discussing although, the sexual actions of most women may appear to be corrupt when judging from a religious perspective. But how could we come to define our women by their sexual urges or interactions because of an examination of what we assume the virtue of appearance should be when it comes to religion. The appearance of an outward aspect and not what's eluded in secret. I'm speaking of the Jezebel who is desirable, alluring, and attractively undeniable but, is referred to as an unchaste woman despite her discreetness.

It's like women are placed under this microscope where they are observed for everything they do. A scope that is mainly used to identify their shame, blunders, and short comings rather than their triumphs. A scope that overlook all that they've achieved or struggled for, just to ridicule or criticize them for not being as capable as men to stand in any position respectfully. It's a scope where opinions don't matter but it's still a rule of the majority.

This is not about actually being a Jezebel, it's about the freedom of unfetter spirits having the choice to do as they please. The right as a married woman to suffice every desire she wish to fulfill, and the individual concerns of a promiscuous woman who yearns for a warm body to lay next to. It's subjective what anyone should think or feel unless it's an indecency to public values or the welfare of other's. I'm talking about the Jezebel we all love but excoriate.

It's the confusion of prostitutes and committed women. The confusion as in there being no difference. We as men tend to believe that majority of women would engage in sex for money. That women can be bought or propositioned for the right price or stake regardless if she walks the streets for prostitution or not. Which is the faultiest belief we could ever presume. Not all women auction their bodies. And not all women are prostitutes. Though many women may have an interest in a male's financial condition, it's more about security, stability, and having a partner who they can depend on or that could meet them half way if necessary, rather than gaining wealth for the benefit of a pimp. And although some women may be more sexually vigorous then most, it doesn't mean that should qualify them as a Jezebel or hoe. A hoe is usually taken out of context. A hoe is considered to be a woman who sale herself as a prostitute for sexual advances. And a Jezebel is a loose woman who sleep with everybody's man. Now if we think a Jezebel to be more than that, then let's say she is a woman who sleeps around period. That would make almost the entire population of women to be a Jezebel because not every married man has wedded a virgin. And I'm quite sure that not every bride has been with less than one person before joining them in union. And women often give their selves to men in hopes to become something more, to preserve their relationship, and to show their commitment. I agree that any other reason should prove otherwise but, there should be a fine line on what stipulates a woman to be a Jezebel. Because without there being any we would always end up pointing a finger at a woman for just wishing to show her devotion. And it shouldn't be a problem with a woman wanting to suffice her needs or enjoy certain pleasures without interfering or affecting others consolidation.

We tend to allow rumors or admissions of the disclosed sexual performance or reputation of women cloud our judgement, and in some cases, causing us to believe that we can treat certain women unworthy and in a defiled manner. For that reason, we mistakenly conclude the misrepresentation of a Jezebel simply because of the unrestrained curiosities a woman erotically seeks to experience in her private life. And whether a woman is deemed to be a Jezebel or not she still deserves the proper respect of a human being. A committed woman is just something I wanted to use as an analogy of a woman who is devoted to a single partner or one who isn't linked to only one man. It's a woman who is committed to the ideal of being pleased but not by soliciting herself in secrecy or publicly. It's a likeness to the women who just wish to enjoy the pleasure of sex without being labeled.

So, women are given the impression that their lack of discretion or disregard for what other's think when it comes to sex is sinful, unlawful or disobedient which causes them to refrain from certain pleasures or become introverted at the thought of being more open to try new things. There is always someone or something intending to be a discouragement for women when it comes to sex, rather then it is for men. Whether it's the fact that she isn't married or has multiple partners. Women are disparaged and criticized at a disproportionate rate compared to men when it comes to sexuality. They can have as many sexual partners as men and be perceived in the most foul and repulsive manner. There has always been a double standard that degrades women but honored men when it comes to sexual content. A standard that again refuses to see women as an equal to men. But how could women be ridiculed, faulted, or branded for what they do in privacy to please their lovers when their accomplices in this censurable behavior doesn't share any blame? And according to who theories should they be the only one judge in the matter?

But the question is whom are thou Jezebel? Is it every woman or does she have to fit a certain criterion? Is she a woman who just wish to feel sexy and dresses in the most enticing manner that gains attention? Is she the sultry woman who flirts suggestively or enjoys seducing men from time to time in order to relieve sexual tension? Is she the woman who refuses to commit herself to one partner or the one just looking for a cheap thrill? Is she the women walking the streets attempting to lure a john? Is she the one sleeping with everyone's man, or is she the one just sleeping with single men from time to time being that she hasn't found the right guy? Is she the devoted wife who is willing to explore sexual heights that isn't considered appropriate? How could we come to judge who are thou Jezebel when we place a figuration on all women that says if they aren't modest in their conduct they're ostentatiously too vulgar for proper refinement. Women are expected to act a certain way, think a certain way, and live a certain way according to moral principles. And they are stereotyped when they exceed the limits of those expectations. Women aren't expected to be forward in the pursuit of sexual relations nor are they expected to have intercourse within a certain time frame of meeting a man. Although, a woman has the ultimate decision whether or not she wish to further things, she isn't allowed to initialize the conversation of sex. Debauchery becomes unbalanced when moderation and intemperance is being weighted by society even though the perception is discriminating. So, it's seemingly fair to say that the views about woman are truly prejudice and lopsided.

Women are considered scandalous and disgraceful if they slept with more than one man. They are thought to have soiled themselves and debased the value of their worth. But the value of their self-worth isn't based on the pleasures they indulge in. It's established by their intellect and productiveness. And their determined ability to stay ambitious in the pursuit of their accomplishments. Just because a woman who may be known to be more sexually adventurous in the bed room then average, doesn't mean she should be despoiled or shamed. And she shouldn't have to be apologetic about her actions at all. Whether she chooses to enjoy the comfort of one or more partners, then what is customarily accepted. It's her exclusive right.

Women are criticized whether they're promiscuous or not. Even if they are sexually restrained and hasn't been willing to try numerous or different techniques of satisfaction, or is unreserved, and has offered themselves fully in the pleasure of sex for their own ecstasy or gratification of the one lover she claims, she is judged. It's as if society always find a reason to discredit their individual or general worth by focusing on what's trivia.

Women are equated with offensive misconceptions by being attached to certain demeaning names that are insulting to their dignity. Names that tends to diminish their quality, character, or position. Women are invectively attacked whether their actions are associated with these disrespectful or sullied epithets or not. Most men have a tendency to resort to misnomers when they are rejected or passed up by a woman who doesn't show any interest in them. Their still viewed as a Jezebel. Why liken women who aren't "loose, fast tailed, or hoes to be more exact" to a Jezebel even when they prove to be reserved? It just goes to show that Jezebels aren't only labelled by unchaste actions but also when a preference isn't suited. And that they often are judged by bitter men, sexist and conservative respective who would normally have separate views but find themselves in concur with this matter because of one's dissatisfaction, the others discrimination, and another's offense due to immoral decorum. Again, showing that women are at a disadvantage when being perceived. But how did they come to be Jezebels?

Society seem to have a problem with publicly acknowledging the sexuality of women. They generally rather their titillating urges to be tamed or suppressed. They psychologically force women to believe that their licentious comportment taints their image. They expect them to live their lives according to what they feel is proper. Due to what they deem is strange or taboo and should cause women to feel embarrassed by their actions. Only to convince them to refrain from exploring sexual heights that would grant them much more pleasure and settle for a life of sexual boredom.

Women are truly the most sexual creatures. Everything about them is seductive from their appearance to the way they move or act. For years they have been conditioned by society to minimize their level of prurient to avoid being labelled a Jezebel. Their expression of free will, activity, or functioning has been bounded by what other's think. Their prohibited of being to explicit or having any wanton desires that are considered extremely lascivious as if their personal life should cause anyone to feel offended. However, they choose to live is their discretion no matter the opinions of other's. and they should never feel threatened or alienated because of their individual preference.

As long as you can live happily with the choices you make, you should never pay any attention to what other's mention or the misperception they view of you. And regardless if your continued to be judged as a Jezebel you're still the most beautiful misconception that has ever been appraised.

Charades

Racist cases of victims of hatred; all whom were killed by ignorance or racist; try to identify the tragic described as I relate the stories of these lost black lives,
Who am I?

On my way home from a convenient store after stepping outside to take a walk being that I was bored; And also, to retrieve a drink and snack in which I brought an ice tea and a pack of skittles before heading back,

I figured I'd take a short cut through the town houses called the retreat at twin lakes where I was sent to visit my dad and his fiancée Brandy Green due to a suspension from Dr. Michael M. Krop High School for a childish mistake,

Strolling along unaware I could be doing any harm or breaking any laws by talking on a phone or having a hoody on; I continued to head in the direction where my family stay,

It appeared as though I was being pursued as I proceeded to move a bit scared and confused thinking I should run as the voice over the phone suggested I do the same after advising my friend that I was being followed by this strange dude; Though I decided to keep my cool hoping this guy who was posing as a sleuth would desist in his pursuit,

Unaware that this so called individual who was selected to be neighborhood watch and given a pistol although he wasn't actually a cop; Had phoned the police about the issue at 7:09 p.m. reporting that a suspicious black guy was peering into people's windows; Possibly with the intent to burglarize which was a lie and didn't make any sense being that I didn't have any tools or nothing in my possession that would convince or give anyone the impression that I would commit that sort of offense,

It seems he took more offense to my presence in the area because of the color of my skin and the fact that I had hoody on which caused his aggressions to become intense,

Despite orders to cease to proceed trailing after me directed by a dispatching officer who gave clear warning; I was still followed by this man who took the law into his own hands and decided he would confront me about my where about before he allowed me to leave,

As if I didn't have the right to be out at night or walk around without being harassed or asked questions about where I should or shouldn't be,

During this interrogation we got into an altercation that became physical as punches flew and we begin to tussle as I fought to get free,

A gun was seen at some point followed by screams for help in which I yelled feeling like my life was threatened though this guy claimed he feared for his himself,

The yells were heard by the neighbors who's homes we were in between; those who heard immediately called the police after being disturbed by the scene they vaguely seen their self,

A shot was fired in which everything became quite; One person was lifeless while the other remained silent; A single bullet to the chest wasn't something I thought would transpire,

Found dead at 7:17 p.m. by police officers eight minutes after the distress call that led to my death for no honest reason except that I was black; And the antipathy of another man which motivated him to act,

A missing person's report was filed by my dad who didn't find me around when he got back home being that he was working late when I left out for a snack,

Only to discover I had been murdered less than a hundred yards down from the town house where we stayed at,
Who am I?

Racist cases of victims of hatred; All whom were killed by ignorance or racist; Try to identify the tragic described as I relate the stories of these lost black lives,
Who am I?

What started out as a night of celebration; As me and a few friends decided to head to club Kalua to enjoy a special occasion,

Unaware that the club owners were under investigation for the accusations of fostering prostitutes which wasn't my perturbation,

We were only there for a bachelor party my friends threw since it was my last night being single; Wanting to relish the moment by getting a lap dance or two and throw a few singles; Not knowing that undercover detectives who were present were focusing more on us rather than their duty that was being neglect; As me and my friends intermingled

After being entertained and having a few moderate drinks; We decided to call it a night as we be begin making our way towards the exist as I started to think how my life was about to change,

Upon stepping outside an argument ensued; Apparently unknown with who; But mentions of a fire arm being used caused me and two of my pals to jumped into my vehicle; Not wanting to stick around to witness a confrontational feud,

As we drove off we were then pursued by an unmarked car which collided into ours; hitting us from the side for no reason at all,

Shaken up by the collision and unable to get out of the driver's side after being ordered to surrender; Due to the damage of the door's condition,

As I sat trapped inside trying to figure out why or what to do; There was an accusation that a gun had been seen or was being retrieved by either my friends or me which was impossible to see from outside of the car even if it was the truth to what was being claimed,

Next thing I knew shots begin to ring as triggers continuously squeezed rattling my automobile as if we were target practice for the N.Y.P.D.,

50 Shots! Fired by the undercover officers at the scene but not one bullet returned by my friends nor me,

No gun was recovered or any "weapon" they had so called seen,

But speculation tried to discourse the fact that I was unjustly slain for no legitimate reason at all,

Instead of meeting at an alter; My wife to be was led to my coffin along with my daughter after my slaughter,

And the accused officers charged was set free by a judge's order?
Who am I?

Racist cases of victims of hatred; All whom were killed by ignorance or racist; Try to identify the tragic described as I relate the stories of these lost black lives,
Who am I?

Out drinking and socializing with two white men who were so called childhood friends that I grew up with in Paris, Texas,

Unaware of any signs of discrimination or their alleged ties to a white supremacist organization; Although they both had criminal records I didn't see a reason to feel threatened,

Especially since we worked the same occupation; Hanging sheetrock on the job and also hanging out on occasions when we clocked off,

But one particular night we were getting wasted; And ended up getting into a minor confrontation about who was less intoxicated; And sober enough to get us to our destination without getting pulled over for a citation,

I guess that was the least of my perturbation; Because being that I wasn't the one who won the argumentation; Even though I felt that both of the other guys had a higher level of inebriation; I decided to get out of the truck and find some other means of transportation,

But as I motioned to go around towards the front; I felt a bump by the grill of the truck; Realizing that the one driving had hit me as my body slumped to the pavement,

Angry and bit frustrated; Figuring they were just horse playing as I laid on the ground feeling parts of my body aching,

Assuming they were going to get out of the vehicle to help me up and let me know it was a mistake and that they were just having fun; But instead was shocked and startled that it wasn't just a stunt as the truck accelerated and I got stuck to the undercarriage as I yelled and pleaded for their cessation,

Unable to make sense of the situation which caused such a horrific demonstration that led to me being ran over and dragged about 40 feet before I was plucked from underneath the chassis; Strewn and mangled bad then forsaken like some worthless trash; Only after two beer cans was emptied on my corpse to add insult to devastation,

At first the incident was ruled as an anonymous hit and run accident that was quack; And due to a botch investigation by local white police officer's both men responsible for my death was set free because of a lack of evidence to support the facts,

Even though traces of my blood were found beneath the defendant's truck that was more than enough clause to charge these men for their sadistic act,
Who am I?

Racist cases of victims of hatred; All whom were killed by ignorance or racist; Try to identify the tragic described as I relate the stories of these lost black lives,
Who am I?

Raised in Alcolu, South Carolina just another young kid who happens to be black,

Living in a small working-class mill town where whites and colored neighborhoods were separated by rail road tracks,

Minding my own business along with my sister Katherine; when two young white girls passing by on bicycles had stopped in front of my families property and begin asking if we knew where they could find maypops at?,

After giving them some directions unaware that I was doing anything wrong or that they would be harmed just because I made a few suggestions in which I was only answering their questions; so that they could move on in quest of the passion flowers they were seeking to obtain,

I returned back to my porch where me and my sister played before they decided to intervene; No longer thinking about where they had gone or who else they had seen,
Once those girls failed to return home a search party was thrown; Which was conducted by Aldler's man company who had over a hundred volunteers that accompanied; Including myself who joined into help locate where they had gone or could possibly be,

During the search we were paired off into two's, so I figured a little conversing would ease the mood at least till we came up with some leading clues or the search was through; In which I confided to the person with me; That I've see both girls earlier that noon,

The next morning both girls were found dead in a ditch filled with muddy water suffering from extensive wounds and trauma to the face and head also in addition to the oldest of the two genitalia having been bruised; before or after they were slaughtered which was extremely sad news,

Not knowing that the harmless information that I had told the other person when we were searching during our conversation would be used against me as justification to accuse me of a crime I didn't do,

After I was arrested and charged for basically giving directions to be honest and the false accusations of murder; My father was fired from his job in retaliation because of our relative connection while the rest of my family was forced to flee the state; Due to the aggression and racist threats that were made apparently because of the nature of our race even though the charges against me were deceptively portrayed and untrue,

So I was left on my own to face this case alone and was manipulated by persuasion and bribed with some ice cream in exchange for a confession of both killings to a deputy officer during interrogation; Whom made these claims to paint me as the villain; Which clearly shows I was just a child who couldn't think; Let alone commit such a horrific act on my own,

Shortly afterwards I was tried and convicted though no recorded statement or physical evidence that linked me to those girls has been presented; Not even my lawyer bothered to call any witness which was expected since he didn't reject to any of the jury selections that seemed to consist of a box full of white supremacist who found me guilty way before the act was committed; And would rather see me subjected to a lynching instead of electrocuted for a sentence,

An 81-day confinement and trial that ended in ten minutes of a deliberated decision,

I was then executed at 7:30 p.m. in 1944 on the 16th; Regardless of my size presenting difficulty in securing me to the frame holding the electrodes or the adult face mask that didn't fit my head; It was still ordered to carry out my electrocution as if nothing seemed convincing,
Who am I?

Racist cases of victims of hatred; All whom were killed by ignorance or racist; Try to identify the tragic described as I relate the stories of these lost black lives.
Who am I?

After leaving the Viksburg's casino alone; I had accepted a ride from a familiar acquaintance I had known; Being that an actual friend of mine who dropped me off earlier wasn't expected to show up to bring me home,

Figuring I'd just accept a lift from him and two other white men who had agreed to taxi me being that I lived in the direction they were supposedly headed in; But instead of dropping me off at my residence they brought me to a remote country road,

Unaware of the intentions they had in mind although I tried to inquire about where were they taking me a few times; But was only told to sit back-relax-and that I was going to be just fine even though my gut feeling didn't agree so,

Upon stopping in the middle of nowhere; I was attacked and forcefully pulled out the back as one of the guys started severely beating me with a bat; While I struggled to fight back unable to escape the assault that was provoked simply because I was black,

You see unknown to me before getting into the truck and ending up here; Was that two of the guys were affiliates of white supremacist; Who met during a jail sentence and joined the racist group for protection to avoid being victims of prison conditions that caused them to feel threatened; And upon their release somehow the tree became connected,

I was knocked unconsciously and hauled around the back of the pickup;
Urinated on and stabbed before having my ankles chained to the truck
and dragged,

1.5 miles the savagely gruesome towing of my body had seemed to last;
While my limbs were shredded bad and littered all over the place along
with my arm and head that were detached after hitting a culvert edge
they passed,

I was further tugged to an African American cemetery where my
remains had been dumped while my murderers joked and laughed,

Two received the death penalty while the one I so called knew was
giving life for his part in the conspiracy even though the punishment
for their acts would never supplant the pain I felt or the grief my family
will forever have,
Who am I?

Charades

THE BREAK DOWN

The stories in this poem were all based on true events that previously or formerly happened. Actual accounts of racism and unjustified killings of black people who were the target of hatred and senseless attacks. There are many cases of injustice committed against black people daily that isn't truly explained or rectified. Cases that either goes unsolved, unpunished or unnoticed. In some of these cases people are given sentences that seems more merciful to the defendants rather than the victims. These cases continue to prove the value of black lives in America or our worth in a court of law. For many years minorities have been neglected by the constitution of government when it comes to their safety, or either felt like a victim of its regulations when they're the ones facing persecution. It seems that every time a black life is taken by an outside race, a duty is served to justify the tragedy more so then it is to make sure that justice is served. But when there's cases of blacks being the accused in a crime committed, persecution is thoroughly sorted. Every government has an organization structure that defines the specific responsibilities of its public officials. And the constitution contains the basic rules and principles by which a state or nation is governed. Constitutional law is the combined record of all the ways in which the constitution had been used to enforce laws and to deal with institutions and problems arising within a nation. So how can we honestly believe that this constitution recognizes us in their policies if we aren't receiving equal consideration when it comes to equity no matter if the violator is a civilian or a figure of authorized status. There are many black lives who were taken by the hands of those who allow ignorance to corrupt their judgement and taint the views they have of other's. Innocent lives that were taken by those who allowed hatred to cover their hearts with a malicious disease that eats away their humanity. I wanted to incorporate something that would be a reminder and continue to bring awareness to discrimination and injustice. Something that would serve as a monument of acknowledgement but as well as a remembrance of what we are up against as black people. These great losses always seem to get a little recognition in the wake of their tragic but are sometimes long forgotten because our urgency to move on. We have a tendency to address concerning issues only succinctly then pushed them to the back of our minds either because we didn't get the result we wanted or being that we no longer wish to face the problem. But our failure to commit to a purpose for change only allows the opportunity for history to repeat it's self over and over again. So, let's not continue to let these black lives die in vain. Let's prevent the same outcome from occurring the next time by staying active in our call for change.

Now the first story is about Trayvon "Benjamin" Martin. He was a 17-year-old African American from Florida raised in Garden Miami. He was visiting his father and his father's fiancèe in Sanford, Florida at the Twin Lakes Retreat area where his father's fiancée had stayed, because of a school suspension at the time of his death. On the 26th February, Mr. Martin went out to a convenience store to purchase some candy and a soda. As Mr. Martin was returning to the Twin Lakes house he decided to take a short cut to get back to the house he was residing at during his visit. The neighborhood he chose to cut through had several complaints of being victimized by robberies that year. George Zimmerman who was a resident of the area and member of the neighborhood watch program, had spotted Mr. Martin walking through the area and phoned the police, claiming that Mr. Martin had looked suspicious. The dispatcher who had received the call had advised George Zimmerman to stand down and desist pursuing after Mr. Martin. George Zimmerman refused the dispatcher orders stating that he wasn't going to let Mr. Martin get away with nothing and making some disturbing comments as well. George Zimmerman confronted Mr. Martin which turned into an altercation with both men struggling to get the upper hand. Moments later during that struggle Trayvon Benjamin Martin was lying dead with a bullet in his chest. George Zimmerman was not charged by the Sanford police at that time because they claim to have found no evidence to refute his claim of self-defense. In Florida the stand your ground law prohibited law enforcement officials from arresting or charging him. But after national media focus on the tragedy, Zimmerman was eventually charged and tried in Martin's death. A grand jury acquitted Zimmerman of second degree murder and of manslaughter in July 2013.

Now I want to just point out a few things. Whether or not the stand your ground law was truly intended for self-defense. In this case how was George Zimmerman the one claiming self-defense when he was directed to desist following Mr. Martin? How could the law protect the life of a murderer over a victim? Self-defense would mean that the victim would be the one who is being pursued or in fear of their life. How could someone who is following another fear their life when they're the ones doing the pursuing? How could it be self-defense in Zimmerman's case? He was clearly warned not to pursue by an official of the state. How could that not be enough grounds to persecute someone who had taken the life of another. George Zimmerman had the gun in which he wasn't legally registered. George Zimmerman pulled the trigger after being instructed not to approach Martin. George Zimmerman initiated the attack by confronting this young boy, so how was it self-defense?

Following Martin's death rallies, marches, and protestation were held across the nation. Petitions calling for a full investigation and prosecution of Zimmerman garnered 2.2 million signatures. A national debate about racial profiling ensued and the governor of Florida appointed a task force to examine the states self-defense laws. 1,000 people attended the viewing of Mr. Martin's remains the day before his funeral, which was held on March 3, 2012 in Miami, Florida. He was buried in Dade-Memorial Park north in Miami. And a memorial was dedicated to Mr. Martin at the Goldsboro Westside Historical Museum, a black history museum in Sanford on July 2013.

The second story is about Sean Bell who was born in Queens, New

York. Sean Bell had attended a night club with a group of friends, which was supposed to be his celebration night for his bachelor party. Sean Bell was due to get married the next day which was only a few hours away from the time he got to the club. The club he went to was allegedly under investigation for prostitution and had a few undercover officers in attendance trying to catch a break in their investigation. During that night two officers had been watching Sean Bell and his friends as they partied and supported Mr. Bell's last night of being a single man. After enjoying himself and becoming exhausted of all the excitement, Mr. Bell and his friends had begun making their exit. Upon leaving the club an altercation broke out with unrelated individuals in which Mr. Bell and his friends entered their vehicles and dispersed the scene. Five under cover N.Y.P.D. officers then followed Mr. Bell's vehicle ramming it from the side causing Sean Bell and his friends to screech off the road. One of the plain clothed under cover claim to have seen a gun before fifty shots was discharged in which a couple of the officers' reloaded to continue the assault. Mr. Trent Benefield and Joseph Guzman who was also in Mr. Bell's vehicle was shot along with Mr. Bell who had died from his wounds. No gun was ever recovered from Mr. Bell's person or anywhere inside the car him and his friends were in. The incident sparked fierce criticism of the police from members of the public and drew comparisons to the 1999 killing of Amado Diallo. Three of the five detectives involved in the shooting had went to trial on the charge of first degree and second-degree manslaughter, first and second-degree assault, and second-degree reckless endangerment, was found not guilty.

How could these officers be acquitted of such extreme conduct, such abuse of authority, or unjustifiable cause? How could they be found not guilty of such excessive shooting when there wasn't any threat or need to discharge their weapon's in this inappropriate and unreasonable manner? Why was the focus on this man who was due to marry his wife to be the next day, instead of the investigation which was the main concern? Fifty shots are an outrageous amount of times to shoot anyone. And being an officer of the law who is supposed to be trained in deescalating a situation before taking other measures only if their life is in danger, which clearly wasn't the case, shouldn't it be a duty to be certain with sound judgement that a gun was acknowledged without jumping to conclusions? Another man's life was taken while injustice goes unpunished.

The third story is about Brandon "Big Boy" McClelland, a black man whose death sparked racial controversy in the city of Paris, Texas on September 16, 2008. McClelland was killed when he was first hit and ran over by a vehicle, then dragged beneath it, perhaps as far as 70 feet. At first, police assumed he was the victim of an anonymous hit-and-run accident. Further investigation revealed that McClelland was last seen alive with two white men, residents Shannon Finley and Charles Ryan Crostley, both of whom had long criminal histories with Finley being accused by the victim's family of having ties to white supremacist groups. McClelland had apparently known Finley and Crostley since they were all children and the two white men and McClelland were considered to be friends who had been working together earlier that evening hanging sheet rock. They all decided to go for some drinks after work, in which the two white men had gotten extremely intoxicated. McClelland insisted on driving being that they had seemed over the level of intoxication. The other two men had refused to allow McClelland to drive causing him to exit the vehicle, to avoid receiving any citations or getting pulled over, and attempted to find other transportation home when they ran him over with their truck.

The killing occurred around 4 a.m. on September 16th, and initially it was declared a hit and run. According to a Free Speech Radio report, authorities told the McClelland family that a gravel truck had killed Brandon. Crostley and Finley had tried to cover up the incident by washing the blood off their truck and hiding it from sight.

It appears to many that not only were Crostley and Finley trying to cover up their malicious act, but that local and state authorities wanted to hide the reality of life for the small Texas city's Black inhabitants. It wouldn't take a search to uncover the racism that exist in Paris, Texas. In 2006, a 14-year-old young Black woman named Shaquanda Cotton was handed down a juvenile court sentence that could have led to her spending seven years in detention for pushing a hall monitor. Many juxtaposed Cottons sentence to that of a young white woman, whom the same judge sentenced to probation for burning down her family home.

A grand jury in the racially troubled northeast Texas town of Paris returned first degree murder indictments Thursday against both of the white men. They both face up to life in prison if convicted of the charges. And is also being investigated for hate crime charges as well. Finley was also indicted for evidence tampering for allegedly attempting to wash McClelland's blood from the undercarriage of the vehicle.

Paris authorities have asserted that the killing had nothing to do with race. Stacy McNeal, the Texas Ranger in charge of the investigation said, "I don't see how it was racial, being as how they were good friends". However, McClelland's family, Black residents of the town and activists with the New Black Panther Party, the Nation of Islam, the NAACP and the Million more Movement believe differently.

The fourth story is about George Junius Stinney Jr. was an African American youth convicted at the age of 14 years old for the murder of two young white girls in Alcolu, South Carolina. He was the youngest person in the United States in the 20th-century to be sentenced to death and be executed.

Stinney was convicted in 1944 in a one-day trial for first degree murder of two white girls by the name of Betty June Binnicker who was 11 years old, and Mary Emma Thamer who was 8. Both girls had stopped by Stinney's family residence to ask for directions to where they could retrieve some maypop flowers. Stinney and his sister were playing outside when the girls stopped by. It's was a kind of flower that the young girls enjoyed but couldn't find anywhere they normally played. Stinney's family resident was located on the other side of some railroad tracks that separated white and black homes.

A search was conducted once the girls hadn't returned home, in which Stinney volunteered to help. During the search Stinney admitted to one of the volunteers he had been paired with, that he had seen both girls earlier that day. The next day the bodies of the two young innocent girls were found, Stinney had been suspected as the killer. His dad was fired from his mill job and his family was threatened and forced to leave town leaving Stinney without any support or legal representation.

After being arrested, Stinney was said to have confessed to the crime. There was no written record of his confession apart from notes provided by an investigating deputy who allegedly persuaded Stinney into confessing. There wasn't any transcript of the brief trial either.

The question of Stinney's guilt, conviction and execution, the validity of his reported confession, as well as the judicial process leading to his execution have all been extensively criticized.

A group of lawyers and activist investigating the Stinney case on behave of his family petitioned for a new trial in 2013, on December 17, 2014 his conviction was posthumously vacated 70 years after his execution, because the circuit court judge ruled that he had not been given a fair trial. He had no effective defense and the Sixth Amendment rights had been violated. The judgement noted that while Stinney may in fact have committed the crime, the prosecution and trial were fundamentally flawed, in a way to still justified his wrongful death.

The last story is about a man by the name of James Byrd who was 54 years old at the time of his death. James Byrd had just gotten out of prison for the murder of a white woman during a robbery. He spent 25 years in prison for the offense. During sometime after his release he was dropped off at the Riverwalk Vicksburg casino in Mississippi where he was last seen. A friend was supposed to pick him up afterwards but, his ride never arrived. So, he hitched a ride with a white man he knew, who was in the company of two other white males at the time. Instead of being dropped off at the designation he had requested to be taken, he was driven to a remote located area where he was brutally beaten and humiliated. Byrd went missing on March 2nd, but his remains weren't found until March 8th hanging from a tree in the woods behind his own home. For more details on this story look into the James Byrd hanging in Mississippi.

These stories were to remind and familiarize people with the hate crimes that are forgotten or unknown to us. The crimes that are often only acknowledged for the moment. There are many Black people who lose their lives annually to ignorance of all kinds. At the time of their deaths we seem to be infuriated with the injustice that's caused, determined to see that justice is sorted our, and are forceful about our demand for change but, after media coverage has shifted their focus and the attention dies down, we no longer seem as resolute in our call for lawfulness or fair treatment. The lost lives seem to be forgotten by all but the families of each victim. I wanted to write something that would show not only the families of these beautiful lives that were taken that we as a people remember but, we still continue to bring awareness to the tragedies we all were faced with as a whole.

The conversation pt 2: A lost era

(elder) So what's up youngster what's the latest?,

(youth) You mean since our last convene? Well; truthfully, I been kind of feeling elated,

(elder) You see I told you just stay serene and your life would begin to pay off with patience,

(youth) Honestly; Not to ruin your felicitation; But I don't know if the path I took meets your qualification,

(elder) What do you mean by that? Aren't we talking about you obtaining an occupation?,

(youth) Kind of sort of; but the job I chose isn't a minimum wage or a check cleared by a big corporation,

It's more of an organization that's not in accord with a few law violations,

(elder) Oh? So, I guess a clever title would give the "street life" a better presentation,

I don't know what better way to say this but; I believe your decision was ignorant and immaturely contemplated,

(youth) Why cause it's not something you would have engaged in?, (elder) No! Because it's something our communities are plagued with,

    Poisoning our own kind with drugs that hinder their motivation,
    Or preventing them from accomplishing their culminating potential of aspiration,
    Not to mention mental instability – the poor health physically – or the families it ruins generally,
    How about the killings over turf wars or respect?,
    Or the hatred over fortune and fame that divide crews – posses – or sets,
    The imprisonment of father's – brother's – uncles – nephew's – or cousin's; did you consider that?
    Did you even consider the fact that your freedom would be something you end up fighting just to get it back?,

(youth) I don't disagree with that but; I can't sit around and hope that one of these employer's call me back,

    I can't hope to feed my kids; I can't hope to be a man if I'm not financially equip,
    I can't hope to survive; I can't hope that somehow, I'll get by,
    I can't hope for anything if I can't make the sacrifices necessary I see fit,

(elder) But the sacrifices for the good and greater cause is what should be your intent,

    Not this! Not a life of crime and malicious offense,

(youth) If this is what supports my family…then as of right now it's the only thing that makes sense,

(elder) But what happens when your actions cost you entrapment? How then would you provide for those lives from the inside?,

(youth) I'll think about that when it comes time; but right now, that's not on my mind,

I'm just trying to make a little money while being wise,

(elder) Intelligence was also assumed by many before you who are now confined,

There's no smarter way or design to get away with such a violation,
Isn't it obvious with the millions of black men in cages?,

(youth) Absolutely!

(elder) Then why repeat the same mistakes that's been the only result no matter how you play it?,

(youth) Well; I'm just trying to make sure my family isn't a victim of starvation no matter the risk or penalization,

(elder) Okay; if it's a choice you adamantly decided on carrying out; I guess it's no changing your decision regardless of my persuasion,

So, I wish you the best and hope this isn't something you live to regret for the remainder of your duration.

P.O.A.P

The Conversation: A lost Era

THE BREAK DOWN

I decided to follow up the first part of this poem with an extension of that conversation called "A lost Era". I wanted to continue "Incertitude" with the decision of a bad choice due to the doubts some young men have about their ability to succeed. I wanted to show how a young man stubbornness and heedlessness could have him making the most irrational decisions. I particularly chose to name this poem The Conversation: A Lost Era because many young men choose to adopt the street code rather then follow constructive advice that would secure their freedom or future. Most young men see an easy way to procure money and forget to weigh out the consequences of their actions. Their forced in some situations to be a man and take on the responsibilities of an adult being that they have a lack of support or guidance. Not many young men have mentors or people in their lives who care enough to aid them aright even if the task is difficult. In this poem I wanted to give an ideal of the proportion of elders who wish to help young men succeed. Those who don't give up although it seems that they're not getting through to them. Those who believe that change comes with diligence and understand that life isn't simple for no one. I wanted to show how young men feel pressured by that lack of fatherhood to become the provider for the family. And end up killing and poisoning their own people just to appear more vicious or opulent. I wanted to show how most elders still try reasoning with younger men even after they've made devastating decisions that are insalubrious. I wanted to show the reality of what's apparent in today society through this conversation and give the reader an actual understanding of the struggle to save our youth in inner city neighborhoods.

Again, I decided to start off the introduction of this poem with a friendly greeting. I wanted to make it clear that even though the last conversation didn't leave off on a good note, there's no animosity or repugnance displayed by the elder. He knows that the young man is just being a teenager and that he must have patience when talking to him. He was just as unyielding as the youthful man himself when he was that age. So, he knows he must be humbler and forgiving. He knew that it wouldn't be easy to reach the young man but, had hoped he had said something that would resonate with in.

The young man feels the need to bring up the fact that, since their last meeting he's been doing well and there haven't been any hard feelings on his end neither. He wanted the elder to know that he could manage on his own without taking his advice. That he's capable of making decisions that would better his situation.

The elder is feeing excited for the young man's happiness. He assumes the best for the young man because he honestly only wished for him to succeed. He is more relieved that he's making wise decisions that are enabling him to be in a fortunate predicament. He notes that with patience, genuine efforts would pay off. And by staying calm in times of panic or difficulty one could make more rational decisions. But the young man feels the need to correct what's presumed by the elder before his actions be misconstrued. He doesn't wish for the elder to be misled. He knows that the path he chosen isn't something the elder would be proud of. He knows it wouldn't meet his standards but, he respects the elder enough to be truthful.

It's something that baffles the elder. He's been under the impression that the young man has been informing him about his success of finding a legitimate job. But he wonders what could the young man have been referring to this entire time?

The young man tries to advise the elder about his pursuit in the most reasonable way he can describe. It's not honestly his intention to let the elder down but he makes known that the job he chose isn't a legitimate occupation at all. He knows that his choice of direction wouldn't be something the elder agree with. He knows it will only lead the elder to scold him and he just wish to receive the most moderate reaction. But he's not only trying to convince the elder, that what he is doing isn't that terrible, he's also trying to persuade himself.

The elder takes his advisement as a form of sarcasm and expresses a bit of sarcasm of his own. He wants the young man to know that he's not incompetent of understanding what he really means. He doesn't actually feel there's a clever title or explanation that could present a reasonable justification of the streets. However, he prefers to reference the term or view "the streets" (which can be taken as drug dealing, gang banging, or other criminal activities), it would never sound appropriate. He doesn't agree with the young man's decision at all and shows his displeasure by being bluntly critical by letting him know how unintelligent his choice was.

The response of the young man after the elder's comment, shows his lack of complete development and childishness. He automatically becomes defensive and young minded. He replies as if the elder thinks he's better then him because he feels the need to question his methods. He doesn't know if he could believe that the elder wants good for him being that he's always being criticized about his actions. He knows that the elder would be more conscious of his choices because he now has more to lose then the young man. And wouldn't consider going down the road of his past mistakes again. But instead of acknowledging his wrong, the young man resorts to the mind frame of a juvenile who wish to compare both their actions.

Instead of letting the young man know that he's made those same mistakes and did choose a path identical to his, he opted to bring awareness on the things that were plaguing the communities. Damaging or destroying the growth of the people who resided there. The grief or the stagnation that's caused. The harms that isn't actually considered by those who choose to live a criminal life style. The general problems this could cause the young man himself. The senseless tragedies that continue to have no logical cause. He wanted him to understand that the cause of his actions can result in dysfunctional family issues (whether it's immediate or family of other's who are hurt by the decisions he makes). He wanted him to know the affect his actions could have and what he can lose behind his ignorance. And the one thing that most offenders regret is losing their freedom or families because of their wrong choices.

The young man acknowledges the destruction his conduct can cause but, due to his lack of options he feels he has no other choice but to pursue the path he chose. He explains his impatience and urgent need to do something in order for his family to survive. And that the impecunious conditions he's in isn't enough to feed his family. This is often the attitude of most young men who struggle with the reality of not being able to provide for their loved ones. At times they don't feel like a man if they're not financially equipped, because society has put pressure on them to believe that they're not a man if they can't take care of their house hold or maintain a certain way of living. It gives them the impression that they must meet an expectation of wealth no matter how it's procured.

The elder advises the young man that sacrifices shouldn't be made by wrong intention. It should be offered for a good cause by good deeds. It should be for improving or furthering one's situation and not dividing families or ruin the ideal of a future. Not something that would eventually prevent him from being the provider for his family.

The young man feels that right now he has no choice but to do what he must in order to make sure that his family don't starve. It's the only thing that makes sense to him literally and financially. And can't place his hopes into wondering if he would get a phone call for occupation. Since he was dealt an unfair hand, he feels like his path was already determined.

The elder wants him to see the consequences of his actions and not just the temporary gain. Though his intention to provide for his family is good, the elder wants to know how will he be able to adhere to those responsibilities from inside of prison? How will he support them then?

The young man has no concerns for the penalty he may be subjected to. Most young men don't consider the punishment of their infractions before their faced with persecution. They only view the reward or pleasure of their indulgence at the time of their offense. They sometimes assume they can be wiser then the last person who was convicted.

The elder knows there's no such thing as being smarter when it comes to criminal intent. He was once that same young person who thought that he could out smart those before him. He thought he could beat the system and avoid confinement as well. But, like millions of others as calculated as they thought they were, found that they weren't as bright as they seemed. And he wanted the young man to know that.

The young man clearly knew that but, it's not what he wanted to believe in order to go through with it. When most young men take on the responsible roles as care taker or provider, they believe that it's their responsibility to make sure that everything is stable. So even if their conscious of their fate, the fact that they are depended on prevents them from recognizing unstable judgement.

The elder wants to know why then if he acknowledges there are consequences that could jeopardize him or his family, why did he take such a path? If he has an ideal of the unfortunate result, why risk your freedom? In which the young man informs him that as long as his family doesn't starve the chance is well worth it. And that any result that occurs doesn't matter as long as he fulfills his duty.

The elder feels that he has said all that he can possibly say to try and change this young man's direction or make him see the potential in himself. And like the first conversation, he left still having hope for this young man as he wishes him well. He just didn't want the decisions he make to end up being something he regrets. But the elder knows that the fate decided for a person life is inevitable and nothing could change its course no matter how hard we try. But we shouldn't ever give up because if there's even just a small possibility it's worth our effort.

War on Drugs

Is it a War on Drugs or is there a War on Us?,

Because the only target seems to be colored minorities who are constantly ending up in hand cuffs,

Shackled in back of a prison bus heading toward a more structured plantation,

Where we aren't strung from trees, but we are hung inside of a court house where the lynching is done effortlessly,

Or should I say legitimately; By judicial racist who collectively work effectively,

Singled out by a caste system that's mainly characterized by mass incarceration,

And responsible for the devastation of black lives and their annulled liberation,

Exposing Politicians who share a correlation with segregationist,

Due to the harsh laws imposed and policies that show bigot regulations,

Discriminating crack convictions because we're black,

And the disparity between people of color and white defendants who receive unparalleled terms for similar conduct supports that fact,

Conspiracy theories – inquiries – and speculation of genocide,

Suspected by those being oppressed; segregated and penalized,

Attacked by the Reagan administration who declared war before crack had become an issue that was generalized,

And suddenly drugs begin to appear in black neighborhoods everywhere; right after being publicized,

Followed by the media racial portrayal of crack being associated with blacks; that was televised,

Stereotyped by images saturated in news articles and magazine prints that made the attack on minorities seem reasonably justified,

"But it was allegedly the War on Drugs that was emphasized",

And why not acknowledge the "press" sensation of black faces being the only race broadcast to show the drug relation,

When it's clear that the target of elimination isn't the crack infestation,

So, you tell me if these are really just accusations or honest statement; Because facts can't be evasive?,

And modern enslavement could be mistaken if blacks weren't mainly in cages,

Or the fact that in less than thirty years the U.S. penal system exploded with drug sentences accounting for majority of its violations,

And inmates that are black make up more than a half of its population,

But studies show that people of all colors use and sell drugs at an incredibly similar estimation,

So how is it that a darker race is receiving a harsher sentence for simple drug convictions?,

Or become cruel victims of a discerning gutless system,

Who legislation allocated $2 billion to antidrug crusades,

That threw a black parade which consist of black slaves; in prison jumpers no better than the rags worn back in the days,

Master's disguised as correctional officers that controls the slave owner's property,

Black workers assisting in the genocide of their own people but all their mindful of is the salary,

No different from the black folk back then that had that porch nigger mentality,

They say he's my brother because we have the same color; but honestly that's the house nigger who is granted special privileges just to watch me,

And the "War on Drugs" is just a cover up to cloak the truth they hope we do not see,

That these rules were put in place so that the black race is disembodied.

P.O.A.P.

War on Drugs

THE EXPLANATION

This poem was something I really wanted to include in this book. It's a real crisis that's seriously affecting all minorities. I wanted to share my thoughts along with some essential facts that is extremely displeasing, outrageous, and troubling. This poem is the first one of the few that I have written an explanation to. I wanted the breakdown to be strictly about the actual events and accounts of the declaration of the drug war. The disturbing truth that has been giving a blind eye by many in the public. And how it ruins more black lives than any other race. I wanted to separate my opinions from substantive information which is more valid and evident. And give readers an honest report of the injustice black people and minorities have been facing pertaining to the so called "War on Drugs". But in this explanation, I wanted to stick to my usual concept and decipher a few lines I wrote.

I decided to start this poem off by asking the question, is there a war on drugs or is there a war on us? I wanted to know who was the target of this so-called war that was declared? Were there actually intentions to abolish the drug epidemic or was the threat much more surreptitious than proclaimed because although the objective was to get the drugs off the streets, it seems to have had a greater effect on blacks and other minorities more than anything. Drugs (specifically crack cocaine) has continued to be bought and sold all across America. But the black Americans are the ones who's being taken off the streets with lengthy prison terms for a small part in this global distribution. We are mostly the ones who are bound by shackles on a prison bus, we are mostly the only ones facing extreme prison sentences, and we are mainly the ones convicted for drugs more than any other group when it's a fact that black and white people use and sell drugs at a similar rate.

These prison institutions are no different from a plantation. If anything, there more well-structured than an actual farm or slave camp. Inmates are given rags to wear, fed slop three times a day, forced to sleep in small cells no bigger than a closet, governed by tyrannical staff who bring their problems to work and abuse their discretion frequently, separated from their families and loved ones, restricted any sexual contact with their women, additionally punished for frivolous behavior whether wrong or right, and a whole bunch of other things that is mentally depriving and demeaning. Not saying that criminals shouldn't be punished for their crimes, but how much punishment should one be subjected to when they're already being stripped of their freedom, family, and lives? Only to be punished during the course of their initial time and afterwards as well when they undergo supervision and more stipulated regulations. But it's shamefully disappointing that black people and minorities suffer from these conditions the most.

Just because we aren't being strung from trees doesn't mean that black people are no longer being lynched. These legislatives have decided to legalize lynching by issuing penalties that suspend black people without actually killing them. These lynches don't take any effort now a days. There isn't any gang of white men holding one helplessly frightened black man down to be roped up and hung. The prison terms black men and women have been receiving for crimes that are treated more lenient when it comes to white defendants, are truly dissatisfying.

This judicial system clearly shows a bias procedure in the way they process cases. From the way police racially, profile when stopping "random" people to the way courts convict, there has been an unfair treatment of discrimination. And collectively this judicial system has been able to effectively ruin black lives without receiving any major back lash about their discriminatory practices.

It's like black people and minorities are the ones who are singled out by this caste system. Instead of the claims to stop the drug infestation, our freedom seems to be once again annulled. After the civil war, southern whites were outraged by the thought of black liberation and didn't believed that black people shared a place amongst white people. It was quoted by an Alabama planter that: "We (meaning white people) have the power to pass stringent police laws to govern the Negroes – this is a blessing – for they must be controlled". Most white people believed that African Americans lacked the proper motivation to work back then, prompting the provisional Southern legislatures to adopt the notorious black codes. These codes were intended to establish systems of peonage resembling slavery. Nine southern states adopted vagrancy laws – which essentially made it a criminal offense not to work and were applied selectively to blacks – and eight states adopted enacted convict laws allowing for the hiring out of county prisoners to plantation owners and private companies. Clearly the purpose of the black codes in general and the vagrancy laws in particular was to establish another system of force labor. Vagrancy laws and other laws defining activities such as "mischief" and "insulting gestures" as crimes were enforced vigorously against blacks. The aggressive enforcement of these criminal offenses opened up an enormous market for convict leasing, in which prisoners were contracted out as laborers to the highest private bidder. Tens of thousands of African Americans were arbitrarily arrested during that period, many of them were hit with court cost and fines, which had to be worked off in order to secure their release. Prisoners were sold as forced laborers to lumber camps, brickyards, railroads, farms, plantations, and dozens of corporations though out the south. White conservatives contemplated ways of putting black people back into slavery. So, they began imposing laws that would subject black people to jail time. These times are no different than those of the past. Today the so-called war on drugs had been their strategy to put us back into slave like institutions. Ronald Reagan, George Bush Se., and Bill Clinton were all contributors to the harsh laws imposed against blacks during their terms of Presidency, intending to appeal to segregationist they are no different from.

During President Barak Obama's term, he shed light on the fact that there was a major discrepancy and concerning disparity in the crack cocaine guidelines. After years of unfair sentencing, he brought awareness on the fact that black and minority crack distributors were getting sentenced at a ratio of 100 – 1 to white cocaine dealers for the same drug that was only in solid form. That meant that minorities were being sentenced 100 times more severely than white people. And still obstinately determined to keep their prejudiced system intact, congress only ruled that the ration be dropped to 18 – 1.

So again, who's the target because facts can't be avoided. Is it the drugs or has it always been people of color? It's hard not to view corrections or institutions as modern enslavement camps when blacks and Hispanics are mainly the ones being held in them. People of color make up majority of the United States prison population as well as the majority being held for drug violations. Legislation funded the war on drugs by all expenses boasting an incarceration rate that is six times greater than that of other industrialized nations. But the desire to fight the drug infestation didn't solve any problem. It only added to the existing problem white segregationist always had with blacks.

Masters disguised as correctional officers that controls slave owner's property is a reference to black people that have always aided slave owners in the oppression of other blacks. Just because the correctional system employs people of various colors doesn't mean that this system isn't founded on racism or discrimination. The people that work in them are no different from the porch slaves back then who were so focused on saving themselves that they lost sight of the reality that they too were considered dispensable property, and less than a human being. They are so worried about trying to survive themselves that a salary means more to them then the improper practices that they take part in. there are black correctional officers who view black inmates no different than the way white Klan's men do blacks period, because they've been trained to think it's criminals and then there's law enforcement. Just as the house slaves thought it was a difference from them and the slaves in the field. To the white slave master, we all were nigger's and nothing more than laborers, which hasn't changed. And it's sad that they don't even realize the cruel and immoral practice that's going on.

The War on Drugs has always been a cover up to hide the truth. This war was more hatred and hostility towards Black Americans then anything. These rules were put in place for us to be disembodied. The only thing that white segregationist seem to hate more than the equality of color people was the abolition of slavery. And for some time, they've been devising a new system of schemes and strategies to return blacks back to servitude, in any form they could. Some of us refuse to believe it or just fail to see it.

War on Drugs

THE BREAK DOWN

This poem was inspired by a book I had read by Michelle Alexander, a law professor and highly acclaimed civil rights lawyer, advocate and legal scholar. Her book is truly informative and essential to black awareness. I decided to focus more on her delivery about the war on drugs that was supposedly launched to terminate the crisis caused by crack cocaine in inner-city neighborhoods. And the harsh policies enforced by politicians who made the War on Drugs the center of their campaigns and Presidency. Instead black people seem to have become the target more so, then the pursuit to abolish the epidemic of narcotics. Most people assumed that the war on drugs is a racist conspiracy to put blacks back in their place of slave like institutions, plague black communities with an incapacitating substance, or to cause the destruction of blacks due to its nature.

In 1982, President Ronald Reagan announced the current drug war, before crack had even became an issue, in the media or a crisis in poor black areas. A few years after the drug war was declared, crack began to spread rapidly in poor black neighborhoods of Los Angeles and later emerged in cities across the country. The Reagan administration hired staff to publicize the emergence of crack cocaine in 1985 as part of a strategic effort to build public and legislative support for the war. The media campaign was a remarkable success. The media was saturated with images of black "crack whores", "crack dealers", and "crack babies' images that seemed to confirm the worst negative racial stereotypes about the penury inner-city residents. In June 1986, Newsweek declared crack to be the biggest story since Vietnam/Watergate, and in August of that year, Times magazine termed crack "the issue of the year". Thousands of stories about the crack crisis flooded the airwaves and newsstands, and the stories had a clear racial subtext. The articles typically featured black "crack addicts", "crack whores", and "gangbangers", reinforcing already prevalent racial stereotypes of black women as irresponsible, selfish "welfare queens" and black men as "predators" – part of an inferior and criminal subculture. In September 1986, with the media frenzy at full throttle, the house passed legislation that allocated $2 billion to the antidrug crusade, required the participation of the military in narcotics control efforts, allowed the death penalty for some drug-related crimes, and authorized the admission of some illegal obtained evidence in drug trials. Later that month, the Senate proposed even tougher antidrug legislation, and shortly thereafter, the president signed the Anti-Drug Abuse Act of 1986 into law. Among other harsh penalties, the legislation included mandatory minimum sentences for the distribution of cocaine, including far more severe punishment for distribution of crack-associated with blacks-that powder cocaine, associated with whites.

The Anti-Drug Abuse Act authorized public housing authorities to evict any tenant who allows any form of drug – related criminal activities to occur on or near public housing premises and eliminated many federal benefits, including student loans, for anyone convicted of a drug offense. The act also expanded use of the death penalty for serious drug-related offenses and imposed new mandatory minimums for drug offenses, including a five-year mandatory minimum for simple possession of cocaine base-with no evidence of intent to sell. Remarkably, the penalty would even apply to first time offenders.

At the time Reagan declared this war, less than 2 percent of American public viewed drugs as the most important issue facing the nation. Reagan's racially coded rhetoric and strategy proved extraordinary effective. As 22 percent of all democrats defected from the party to vote for Reagan. The defection rate shot up to 34 percent among those Democrats who believed civil rights leaders were pushing too fast.

The timing of the crack crisis helped to fuel conspiracies theories and general speculation in poor black communities that the war on drugs was part of a genocidal plan by the government to destroy black people in the United States. This view holds that the racial disparities in drug convictions and sentences, as well as the raid explosion of the prison population reflect nothing more than the government's resolute efforts to address rampant drug crime in poor, minority sections. And the odd coincidence that an illegal drug crisis suddenly appeared in the black community after – and not before – a drug war has been asserted. In fact, the war on drugs began at a time when illegal drug use was on the decline. During this same time period, however, a war was declared, causing the arrest and convictions for drug offenses to skyrocket, especially among people of color.

In Reagan's campaign for the presidency, he mastered the "excision of the language of race from conservatives' public discourse" and thus built on the success of earlier conservatives who developed a strategy of exploiting racial hostility or resentment for political gain without making explicit reference to race. Condemning "Welfare queens" and criminals "Predators". As one political insider explained, Reagan's appeal derived primarily from the ideological fervor of the right wing of the Republican Party and "the emotional distress of those who feared or resented the Negro, and who expected Reagan to somehow keep him in his place or at least echo their own anger and frustration. In 1964, he assured the crowd of Neshoba county fair near Philadelphia, Mississippi, that he believed in states' rights and promised to restore to states and local government the power that properly belonged to them. His critics promptly alleged that he was signaling a racial message to his audience, suggesting allegiance with those who resisted desegregation. Crime and welfare were Reagan's most favorite and often repeated anecdotes. The story of a Chicago "welfare queen" with 80 addresses, 12 social security cards, "whose tax-free income alone is over $150,000. The term "welfare queen" became a not so subtle code for "lazy, greedy, black ghetto mother".

When Regan was elected, his promise to enhance the federal

government's role in fighting crime was complicated by the fact that fighting street crime has traditionally been the responsibility of state and local law enforcement. After a period of initial confusion and controversy regarding whether the FBI and the federal government should be involved in street crime, the justice department announced its intention to cut in half the number of specialists assigned to identify and prosecute white-collar criminals and to shift its attention to street crime, especially drug-law enforcement. Practically overnight the budgets of federal law enforcement agencies soared. Between 1980 and 1984, FBI antidrug funding increased from $8 million to $95 million. Department of defense antidrug allocations increased from $33 million in 1981 to $1,042 million in 1991. During that same time period, DEA antidrug spending grew from $86 to $1,026 million, and FBI antidrug allocations grew from $31 to $181 million. By contrast, funding for agencies responsible for drug treatment, prevention, and education was dramatically reduced. The budget of the National Institute on Drug Abuse for example, was reduced from $274 million to $57 million from 1981 to 1984, and antidrug funds allocated to the Department of Education were cut from $14 million to $3 million.

Some countries faced with rising drug crime or seemingly intractable rates of drug abuse and drug addiction chose the path of drug treatment, prevention, and education or economic investment in crime-ridden communities. Portugal, for example, responded to persistent problems of drug addiction and abuse by decriminalizing the possession of all drugs and redirecting the money that would have been spent putting drug users in cages into drug treatment and prevention. Ten years later, Portugal reported that rates of drug abuse and addiction had plummeted, and drug-related crime was on the decline as well. Numerous paths were available to us, as a nation, in the wake of the crack crisis, yet for reasons traceable largely to racial politics and fear mongering we chose war.

The War on Drugs proved popular among key white voters, particularly whites who remained resentful of black progress. Reagan's successor, President George Bush Sr., did not hesitate to employ implicit racial appeals, having learned from the success of other conservative politicians that subtle negative referenced to race could mobilize poor and working-class whites who once were loyal to the Democratic party. Bush most famous racial appeal, the Willie Horton ad, featured a dark-skinned black man, a convicted murderer who escaped while on a work furlough and then raped and murdered a white woman in her home. The ad blamed Bush opponent, Massachusetts Governor Michael Dukakis, for the death of the white women, because he approved the furlough program. For months the ad played repeatedly on network news stations and was the subject of incessant political commentary. Though controversial, the ad was stunningly effective; it destroyed Dukakis's chances of ever becoming president. Once in Oval Office, Bush stayed on message, opposing affirmative action and aggressive civil rights enforcement, and embracing the Drug War with great enthusiasm. In 1989, President Bush characterized the drug use as "the most pressing problem facing the nation". Shortly thereafter, a New Your Times/CBS News Poll reported that 64 percent of those polled – the highest percentage ever recorded – no thought that drugs were the most significant problem in the United States.

The surge of public concerns did not correspond to a dramatic shift in illegal drug activity, but instead was the product of a carefully orchestrated political campaign. The level of public concern about crime and drugs was only weakly correlated with actual crime rates, but highly correlated with political initiatives, campaigns, and partisan appeals. The shift to a general attitude of "toughness" towards problems associated with communities of color began in the 1960's, when the gains and goals of the Civil Rights Movement began to require real sacrifices on the part of white Americans, and conservative politicians found they could mobilized white racial resentment by vowing to crack down on crime. By the late 1980s however, not only conservatives played leading roles in the get-tough-movement, spouting the rhetoric once associated only with segregationist. Democratic politicians and policy makers were now attempting to wrestle control of the crime and drug issues from Republicans by advocating stricter anticrime and antidrug laws – all in an effort to win back the so-call "swing voters" who were defecting to the Republican Party. Somewhat ironically, these "new

Democrats were joined by virulent racists, most notably the Ku Klux Klan, which announced in 1990 that it intended to "join the battle against illegal drugs" by becoming the "eyes and ears of the police". Former allies of African Americans-as much as conservatives-adopted a political strategy the required them to prove how "tough" they could be on "them", the dark-skinned pariahs. The results were immediate. As law enforcement budgets exploded, so did prison and jail populations. In 1991, the Sentencing Project reported that the number of people behind bars in the United States was unprecedented in world history, and that one fourth of young African American men were now under the control of the criminal justice system. Despite the jaw-dropping impact of the "get tough" movement on the African American community neither the Democrats nor the Republicans revealed any inclination to slow the pace of incarceration.

In 1992, President candidate Bill Clinton vowed that he would never permit any Republican to be perceived as tougher on crime than he. True to his word, just weeks before the critical New Hampshire primary, Clinton chose to fly home to Arkansas to oversee the execution of Ricky Ray Rector, a mentally impaired black man who had so little conception of what was about to happen to him that he asked for the dessert from his last meal to be saved for him until the morning. After the execution, Clinton remarked, "I can be nicked a lot, but no one can say I'm soft on crime". Once elected, Clinton endorsed the ideal of a federal "three strikes and you're out" law, which he advocated in his 1994 state of the Union address to enthusiastic applause on both sides of the aisle. The $30 billion crime bill sent to President Clinton in August 1994 was hailed as a victory for the Democrats, who "were able to wrestle the crime issue from the Republicans and make it their own. The bill created dozens of new federal capital crimes, mandated life sentences for some three-time offenders, and authorized more than $16 billion for state prison grants and expansion of state and local police forces. Far from resisting the emergence of the new caste system, Clinton escalated the drug was beyond what conservatives had imagined possible a decade earlier. Clinton eventually moved beyond crime and capitulated to the conservative racial agenda on welfare. It was part of a strategy articulated by the "new Democrats" to appeal to the elusive white swing voters, like his "get tough" rhetoric and policies. Clinton-more than any other president – created the current racial undercast. He began passing bills that ended welfare and the grants that would aid families with dependent children. He imposed a permanent lifetime ban on eligibility for welfare and food stamps for anyone convicted of a felony drug offense – including simple possession of marijuana.

The government began to alter the money devoted to management of the urban poor. Similarly, funding that had once been used for public housing was being redirected to prison construction. The dramatic shift toward punitiveness resulted in a massive reallocation of public resource. During Clinton's tenure, Washington slashed funding for public housing by $17 billion (a reduction of 61 percent) and boosted corrections by $19 billion (an increase of 171 percent), "effectively making the construction of prisons the nation's main housing program for the urban poor. Clinton also made it easier for federally assisted public housing projects to exclude anyone with a criminal history – an extraordinarily harsh step in the midst of a drug was aimed at racial and ethnic minorities. In his announcement of the "one Strike and You're Out" Initiative, Clinton explained: "From now on, the rule for resident's who commit crime and peddle drugs should be one strike and you're out. The new rule promised to be "the toughest admission and eviction policy that HUD has implemented. Thus, for countless poor people, particularly racial minorities targeted by the drug war, public housing was no longer available, leaving many of them homeless.

By the mid-1990s, no serious alternatives to the War on Drugs and "get tough" movement were being entertained in mainstream political discourse. More than 2 million people found themselves behind bars at the turn of the twenty-first century, and millions more were relegated to the margins of mainstream society, banished to a political social space where discrimination in employment, housing, and access to education was perfectly legal, and where they could be denied the right to vote.

The system functioned relatively automatically, and the prevailing system of racial meaning, identities, and ideologies already seemed natural. Ninety percent of those admitted to prison for drug offenses in many states were black or Latino, yet the mass incarceration of communities of color was explained in race-neutral terms, an adaptation to the needs and demands of the current political climate.

Listen

Just listen because ignorance is bliss,

And negligence is idly expended when you're trying to make sense,

And an immanent solution prevents conducive intent because of the lack of intelligence,

And what's come to pass is now useless; so, what you should have knew is irrelevant,

And a resolution can't be resolved being you refused beneficial advice you assumed wasn't evident,

No clue how to pursue the issue without comprehension that's relevant,

So, you rely on intuition for a decision that requires some serious delving,

Common sense isn't always prudent or construed discerning elements,

But erudition eliminated confusion and assures pressing development,

So just take a second to listen when wisdom is presented; and life's answers wouldn't cause so much intentional puzzlement.

P.O.A.P

Listen

THE BREAK DOWN

This poem is actually a part two to choices. A lot of the poems I create are often worthy of sequels due to the nature of the topic I'm trying to convey. And choices are definitely one of those poems, but instead of expressing my concerns through the eyes of a student I wanted to address the class room from the perspective of a teacher this time. While explaining the concept of choices I conveyed an ideal of being in a class of life and being negligent in the lessons you are presented. But this poem is more like a demand for the attention of every mind in attendance. It's still that class room setting but it's more from the teachers of error's who are now wiser than they were in their past. And the teachers of faultlessness who lived correctly. Their decisions are more intelligent than they use to be. And they are more aware of the importance of their choices. I wanted to kind of compare the teachers inside a school building with the teachers who gained their knowledge in the streets. Both of them feel they have a job to provide the best guidance. To equip the youth with the tools that's going to help them succeed in life and not ruin them. This poem is about the concerns of a teacher who wished to get through to the student who has their life ahead of them but is at a point where their decisions could better or worsen their lives. This poem is like that teacher in the class room who has been ignored, disrupted, and treated like they must earn the respect of the students who are un co-operative, to get their attention. Sort of like what happens to many substitute teachers who must fill in for the steady. This is like seeing that substitute putting their foot down and taking control of the disorderly and interruptive conduct of the class room. And Just saying "listen!". I wanted to depict that teacher standing up there speaking eloquently confident and forcefully grabbing the attention of the students in the most captivating way through my poetic expressions of conscious advice.

The teacher starts by saying just listen because ignorance is bliss. Remember these are two types of teachers that's doing the lecturing. And that admonishment in the poem choices, the student was telling his peers to take heed to the advice. This was the advice that he was warning them to take notice of. Now anyone could settle for ignorance because it doesn't require any effort. It's something that comes naturally easy due to the modicum of energy it takes to make an uneducated decision. And who doesn't take pleasure in doing something that isn't difficult? It's comfortably fun when you don't have to apply yourself to something that causes mental strain or pressure. There's no learning guide on how to be ignorant. And no one has ever had to study to be illiterate. Ignorance could seem fun and harmless when people lack real concerns. It could be your joy now, but the later outcome won't turn out to be a smart result. And both types of teachers know this because either they were once in the same predicament of making bad choices or they're a great example of how making the right decisions could turn out. Being a delinquent is uselessly spent when you're trying to make "sense". Time can idly be wasted on unproductiveness when a person neglects their duties. But when I mention the word "sense", I'm actually referring to two different meanings. The first "Sense", being the intelligence to decide the most effective decisions. And the second "Sense", I'm talking about trying to make cents as in money, by going about making the wrong choices in a miscreant manner just for personal gain. If knowledge is being treated as unworthy of notice or regard when planning your life, then understanding the science that deals with the rules and tests of sound judgement gets extremely unsteady when you refuse to take heed. Meaning, the knowledge covering general truths behind the actions that test your judgement can be unstable if you fail to understand the seriousness of your volition.

A knowledgeable solution can't be resolved if an individual lack intelligence. You can't expect to make the right choices if you prevent yourself from having the mental capability to think wisely in your decisions. If you haven't yet received any knowledge or experience, how could you ever feel equipped to make the right determination. Lacking awareness prevents us from contemplating better possibilities or contributing to a brighter outcome.

We all must become teachers sooner or later in life and provide monition to the next generation that needs our guidance. No one remains a student forever unless you continue to fail miserably. Even then you would probably end up being discharged if you're too far behind. In life and in school we all advance when we follow instructions and pay attention to what's being taught. The more we learn the more we get ahead. And that's the same thing with life. The more we learn how to avoid stagnation or hindering problems, we would always proceed to progress or excel. When we do make it to that point where we are the ones teaching, we should rather to become the teacher who's in a more suitable position. We don't want to end up like the teacher who has a life full of regrets and has waited too late to take heed to the advice that was given. Because what's come to pass is now irrelevant for those who have already wasted their lives. And though what they once knew no longer benefit them, it could still be of use to someone else. But we shouldn't want for our mistakes to only serve as someone else's warning or gain. We should want better for ourselves as well. We should want to be that teacher who takes pride in their studies and has equipped them self with the proper knowledge to pass on. If you don't think that the advice given is evident now, how could you live with being unmindful to what's salubrious for us when life proves you misjudged the circumstances? And if you don't have a clue how to pursue the adversity you face without it being perspicuity, when it matters, how can you then find a resolution that would optimize your situation. Especially without laboriously seeking information that could help and not going off intuition or conjectures.

One thing for certain is that, common sense isn't always sound or could be recognized mentally even with an interpretation representing the translation of one's conditions. Often people see that they have poor judgement and continue to make the same mistakes because they refuse to learn. But when they do begin to ascertain the right fundamentals that assures pressing development, it eliminates any vagueness or confusion as to what's important when figuring out what to decide. So just take a second to listen when insight is offered because the time you devote to a wise attitude or course of action can spare a person of making fewer mindless blunders in their life. We must understand that the classes of life aren't a school for dereliction. We can graduate to a prosperous life or we can demote ourselves to an unproductive living. But any advice could prevent unfortunate choices that ruins part of your life or all of it.

A Child's Mind

A child's mind is young and naive,
Sometimes gullible and open to be deceived,

Easy to mislead because his or her conscious is eager to receive,

Ready to be guided by the interest that leads,

Wanting to be a part of something that makes them feel consolidated or in most cases essential to whatever need.

Underestimating the possibilities or devastating situations that impedes,

Because it's a child's mind,
Designed to develop throughout time,

Enhancing due to evolutional improvement where maturity supplants any youthful signs still looming,

It gets tricky,
Because some of us are stuck in our childish ways,

As if our inner child was suppressed from transcending to an adult stage,

Keeping our minds trapped in that childhood phase,

Where thoughts refuse to grow up to assume the responsibility of the correct choices that should be made,

So, the way the child mind behaves is sort of like the actions a delinquent kid display,

And the parent is providing admonishment to prevent them from being a prisoner of the state,

Or crucified in the streets they reside causing fear – terror – and hate,

Because they don't listen, or you've told them too many times to the point you just wanted them to learn from their ignorance to see why you try to keep them safe,

And despite parental guidance or advisement it's deviant desire to defy the obligation it has to be reliant is always a headache,

Because when repeating the same lectures or taking certain measures so that discipline could make them better sometimes cause of lack of faith,

So, it may seem that expecting a grown child to change is a waste,

Because if they're still making the same mistakes,

It's apparent that mentally for them it's probably too late to make the fully developed decisions of an accountable human being that has already attained a mindful state,

Which would help them chose the right circumspection when determining the case of their fate,

But this is a child's mind we are considering,

And it's the parent brains duty to make sure that the immaturity isn't something that continues to be hindering no matter what it takes.

P.O.A.P

A Child's Mind

THE BREAK DOWN

Now this poem was meant to be the first version of the distinguish between the parent brain and the child's mind. More so, the distinction of a thinker and the absent-minded person. Instead of making the parent brain part two of this edition I just wanted to give each poem their own acknowledgement but still as if they were correlational because they are. You can't have a parent brain if you don't know what negates it to be the responsible one. Just as you can't recognize a person who possess a child mind if you don't know what affirms or validate its improvements. I wanted to point out the characteristics of a childish minded individual. One who ceaselessly makes the most immaturely and absurd decisions. Decisions that are mostly irrational and illogical. Often unaware of the harm or danger in his choices and is foolishly committed to its longing desires more then it's wellbeing. A person who doesn't actually regard the consequence in whatever matter that's considered. One who is neglectful of their obligation to be more reliable or accountable. It's everything that defies the traits of having sound judgement. I wanted to make the comparison of a child mind "being a kid" and a child's mind "being one who is capable of understanding but thinks like a kid". In the sense of being a delinquent, being careless, and not having a responsibility that governs their actions. Because the child's mind and a child mind have some of the same psychological characteristic's although a child mind still has the ability to grow. This poem is titled the child's mind due to a person's inability to think sagaciously.

It's known that a child mind is feeble. It's easy to be manipulated or become persuaded by whatever influence it finds an interest in. It's inclining to believe that which has no merit because of its failure to acknowledge the difference between right and wrong and is quick to be deceived do to its lack of awareness. The child's mind is the same way. It's very gullible and eager to receive any guidance do to its willingness to fit in or please other's. Especially if that guidance doesn't require any regulations that bound this kind of a person to an obligation to be dependable. It's something that isn't manageable due to its irresponsibility and heedfulness. It's young, meaning that it isn't mature enough to make careful decisions. It's hasn't developed mentally or grew to the point of sensibility. It's incapable of making precise judgement that prevents disaster or misfortune. And is unconscious of the damage it truly causes other's or itself.

Let me further elucidate about the child's mind being eager to receive. Just like a kid who is learning, the child mind also possesses the ability to be receptive to information as well. But unlike the actual kid who is fascinated with becoming familiar with all understanding, the child mind has disregarded the essential things more substantive to its existence and also what's intelligently correct. It has only made room to retain the things that is mostly intended to grant instant gratification instead of long term security. It's eager to receive as long as what's being provided is within the lines of what it is willing to accept. It's ready to be guided by the interest that leads. And in most cases that interest can be destructive. It has no problem following a frivolous cause or purpose due to its lack of interest in that which is fundamental or vital. It's almost like those who join gangs or groups of individuals who guide those who are uncertain with who they are or their purpose in life, in a direction that isn't favorable, or has a woeful outcome. But their determination to be a part of something that makes them feel consolidated and essential to a need or cause, despite their neglect for what's salubrious, makes them unconscious of the threat they serve.

The child's mind tends to underestimate the possibilities or deviation regarding any situation. It never contemplates the severity in a matter with great extent. It never ponders the endangerment with extreme consideration. It only sees the satiation of what's desired with excessive want. And like a child, those same traits can be found. A child isn't aware of the greater harm in his/her actions. It doesn't know that there could be a penalty for their error's. And that's because unlike the child's mind the child isn't quite familiar with the probabilities he/she has as a choice.

Because it's a child's mind, it's designed to develop and grow through out time. It's created to increase in knowledge, understanding, and evolve to the point of lucid awareness of its speech and actions. It's made to identify the distinguishes between poor choices and those that are wise after recognizing the difference in what's morally accurate. And enhance when improved by the maturity which forcefully replace any youthful personality that still exist. But it gets tricky because although it's supposing to supplant the childish mind frame some of us display, many of us continue to be stuck in between those adolescent stages of our life refusing to let go of our youthfulness. It's almost as if our inner child is caught up in some kind of suppressing contraption that is preventing us from transcending to an adult state. So, we continue to be trapped in the childhood phase of immaturity where our thoughts are declining to grow up to adhere to the responsibility of making the correct choices that should be made. Leaving us stuck in a period of time where we are still making uneducated mistakes because of our fear of becoming accountable for what we do or who we supervise.

The way the child mind behaves is sort of like the actions a delinquent kid display. It continues to take risk and chances because it truly believes that it can avoid trouble. It never takes the time to consider its consequences because it does not feel that it can be held accountable for the things that are calamitous. It never takes a situation as serious as it should. It believes that it can elude punishment as long as its opprobrious actions are not detected. And the parent, which is the parent brain, is the one always providing admonishment to prevent certain penalties or discipline so that the child mind doesn't end up a prisoner of the state. Which could be incarceration or confinement to an ignorant mentality that repeats the same blunders. The blunders that would have him crucified in the streets he resides. Meaning the mistakes that could cause him/her harm because of whatever inadequate condition their living in. And it also is a reference to being shot up in a cross fire or becoming an illusion of sacrifice for its comrades due to a commitment to a useless cause. And fate is an honest reality because the child's mind doesn't listen to the warnings or lectures given by the parent brain. It's too stubborn to see the helpful concerns in the advice presented. And just as a parent who is always advising a child of their wrong, the parent brain sometimes feel as if it has warned the child's mind too many times, to the point he just wants it to learn from the mistakes that's made, in order to see why he's been trying to keep the child's mind safe. But despite parental guidance or advisement the child mind possesses a deviant desire to defy the obligations it must be a reliant thinker. It's kind of in the child's mind nature to deny such a requirement. It becomes rebellious in a sense to actual enlightenment that could cause germination or bring the child's mind out of a state of being cost defective. Which can begin to take a toll or become a burden to those who are constantly running to their aid. And when repeating the same discussion over and over or taking certain measures to ensure that it's conduct improves, could cause a lack of faith or belief that they'll ever change.

So, it could be a waste of time expecting anything different from a grown child, who is an adult that still makes the same poor choices it has been making since a youth. Because it's apparent that mentally for them it's probably too late to make the rational decisions that any other capable or fully developed human being who has attained awareness, would make. It may be too late to expect them to take accountability for the things that are inexplicable to them. The things that assures that the volition they make isn't defaulted. And the things that would help them choose the right circumspection when determining the case of their fate. But we always must be mindful that this is a child's mind we are considering. And it's the parent brain's duty to make sure that the immaturity isn't something that continues to be a hindrance regardless of how difficult it seems to get through to it. Because although it is a child's mind, it's still needs that genuine nourishment only a parent brain can provide.

Black man why I hate my self

PART 2

Black man why I hate myself is what I inquired for the second time as the mirror begin to say to me,

Is it because of slavery? The maiming – burning – lynching?,

Or maybe it could be the raping of thousands of our black women?.

The tainting of our image? The killing of millions?,

The miseducation of minorities? The discrimination from Caucasians and racial profiling from authorities?

The lost history of a black society? The false teachings and similar preaching's of the ones my ancestors had provided for me?,

How about the years spent on the plantation?
Segregation – manipulation – or degradation?,

The 3/5 of a man you sum up to in the U.S. constitution? Or the aid in making the bondage of the negro's universal and eternal in the declaration?,

The oppression – transgressional pain afflicted from whips and chains?,

Disdained by savage beast with civilized claims but practice imperialism?

Still I don't get why "I" hate myself black man,

It's because you refuse to listen,
Taught to be inferior to white supremacist for so many years that your now immune to those conditions,

Mentally damaged by stereotype vulnerability,

The hostile and heinous acts of race crime up to this day there hasn't been any unity with in the black community,

So why should you love the color of your skin said the image depicted before me?,

When all your doing is adapting to the land of opportunity; the free; and the new home to which slave owners brought thee.

P.O.A.P

BLACK MAN WHY I HATE MY SELF

PART 2

THE BREAK DOWN

In this second poem of Black Man Why I hate My Self, I wanted to show the troubling things we often focus on the most which seems to be affecting our growth. The past ignorance of other's that continues to suppress our future being that we still hold on to those atrocious memories. I wanted to point out the things that we as black people are sometimes quick to use to justify our actions and conduct. The past iniquitous comportment that has continued to be an excuse for our unreasonable behavior or conditions. In this face to face conversation with one's self, I wanted to show a person being confronted by his conscious state who points out the possible reasons he could feel such loathe for his own people. I wanted to give an ideal of a true hypocrite. The hypocrite that resides with in a person who finds fault in others for their misconduct but carry themselves in the same manner. And through the self-image I wanted to convey this false portrayal.

I wanted to start this poem off with just another introduction with the self-image. Again, the questioner seeks answers for the self-hatred that has become a tragic reality. Again, he looks deep within himself for guidance.

During the soul searching the reflective self begins a list of duplicitous questions that could be the problem as to why the actual person himself may have developed this self-hatred for his own people. Is it because of this practice of slavery which forced us to be owned by white slave masters? Is it because we were once viewed as property? Is it the fact that we're no longer considered to be real estate that we feel the urge to cause damage or ruin to each other? Are we now viewing ourselves as disposable chattel? In 1662 Virginia legally recognized slavery as a hereditary lifelong condition.

The comprehensive code outlined severe penalties for a variety of offenses committed by blacks and excused any whites who caused the death of a slave while carrying out a punishment. So was it the maiming – burning – or the lynching that was committed against our black brother's back then that caused us to hate each other. I wanted to raise the question as to why and how could we participate in this cruelty against our own people? Is this the reason: Are we just psychologically condition to punish ourselves now?

Is it the raping of thousands of our sisters that cause us to treat women poorly or as if their worth has no value? Was this the start that trigger our abusive misogynistic behavior? Degrading our sister's and treating them as idle property to be used at our disposal? Belittling their abilities and status to make them seem insignificant or unsuitable to share a place, a voice, or acknowledgement as an essential contributor in the furtherance of our culture? Where did we lose sight of the importance of black women?

The tainting of our image is referring to the contamination of who we are. The way we're perceived. And our great achievements that were supplanted in order to keep us in despondency or despair. A lot of accomplishments that has been acquired by black people had been over shadowed, under rated, or over look to keep us unmotivated. To keep us from being inspired enough to change our fate. Or wanting better for ourselves being that we have no reason to believe that we can accomplish greatness. Or is it the killing of millions that cause us to re-enact those awful heinous tragedies that has come to pass? Is that what drives us to kill our own race? Have we become that immune to the annihilation of our own people that we can't envision life any other way for us? That we can't see ourselves living in peace and harmony?

Could it be the destruction of our inheritance? The abolishment of our true identity and history that was stripped from us? We have been Americanized to the point that any traces of traditions or African customs no longer exist? We were forced to relinquish or abolish our way of life. And give up our beliefs and practices just to conform to the American way. We are miseducated in our ancestor's way of living and cultural observance. Black people are so far from relating to those slaves that were forced to come here, that it's impossible to ever know our true selves. But is that the reason we hate each other? Is that the reason we don't know our brother or sister's well enough to show them love instead of enmity? Are we miseducated to the point that we don't see any place for us in their society? Were we miseducated to the point that we learned how to be each other's enemies because that's the only thing at the time that was ascertainable? Is it the discrimination from racist or authorities? Is it the image of only white signs that still resonates? The unequal demonstrations that made us feel outcaste or inhuman? Or is it the brutal police attacks and racial profiling back then and now, that cause us to believe that we have no right to be treated like citizens or human beings? Did that traumatize us in a way that we feel we don't deserve to be here? That we feel we shouldn't even give our own selves a chance? "Selves" as in race.

The lost history is the false knowledge that was recorded. For years the history of blacks was replaced by white perspectives. Or simply just wasn't acknowledged. From our inventions to our impelling victories. Our faces weren't recognized as some of the great contributors to this society because we weren't deemed worthy or considered good enough to share a part in this nation's history. Like the air conditioner unit design that was created by Frederick Jones, the baby carriage-safety leveler by William Richardson, the computer-world's fastest and the weather forecasting-computerized by Philip Emeagwali, geometry by Tacokoma-calculus by Tishome-and algebra by Ahmes, heart (open heart) surgery by Dr. Daniel Hale Williams, and the statue of liberty by Edourd de Labooulaye. Just to name a few of the things we weren't recognized for. You can find more of our uncredited contributions at www.avengingtheancestors.com. But was that reason enough for us to want to be viewed as a race that destroyed itself? Is this our way of making history? We were taught to perceive things through the American perception. We were given the American account of the way things transpired, the events that took place, or was recorded. Or wasn't acknowledge at all for our assistance in shaping this country to what it is. But did this cause us to teach our selves that our lives don't matter? That we will never be acknowledged? That no matter what we do we would never be good enough?

Was it the plantations? The humiliation of planting and picking cotton by manual labor? Wearing tow-cloth and coarse shoes that was presented probably yearly? Living in hog huts, huddled like cattle? Bedspreads or furniture that were made of rags? Being housed in worse conditions then a pig? Having no rights? The lashings or short rations provided? The selling of family to other slave owner's? Was it those living arrangements that made it impossible for us to live with each other?

Many black labors gradually replaced white indentured servants as the principle source of agricultural labor during half of the 17th century. Law restricting the activity of Africans were being introduced codifying slavery as a rare based system. South Carolina for example, passed an Act for the better ordering and governing of slaves in 1696. The South Carolina Act was based upon the slaves of Barbados and became the prototype for other American colonies writing black oppression into law.

Was it the division, the deception or belittlement which kept us obedient as slaves? Those deceitful tactics that forced us to comply. Was it those things that made us hate who we are? Hate the sight of one another?

In the U.S. Constitution a black man or woman only sum up to 3/5 of a person. It was part of the original text. It appeared in article one, section two, paragraph three. It was one of the three passages in the constitution that acknowledged the existence of slavery and gave special privileges to slave owners, without actually using the word "slave" or "slavery". The three-fifths clause gave slave states more power than free states in the house of representatives. Some of the delegates to the constitution convention wanted to determine each states population by counting just the free citizens in that state. Slaves couldn't vote and representatives from slave states would be representing the interests of slave owners, not the interest of slaves. So counting slaves as part of the population when figuring how many representatives a state would get was a way of giving extra power to slave owners. The decision to count three-fifths of slaves for that purpose was a compromise between those who wanted to count them all and those who didn't want to count any. We weren't granted any rights as an individual. The constitution of what this county is founded upon didn't even acknowledge us as a complete human being. We weren't considered citizens of the United States. And we weren't considered or treated as people to those who were. But is that grounds not to considered each other as human beings or acknowledge our brother's and sister's as a person? What about the aid to make the bondage of Negro's universal and eternal in the declaration of independence? Slaves didn't have the luxury of free pursuit of labor or was compensated for their hard-earned work like everyone else. Early Americans embraced a universal moral system rooted in free labor but, Lincoln economic and antislavery views merged to cast a grand vision, tying the moral bankruptcy of bondage to the dream of economic opportunity. In other words, it was hard for people (specifically in the east) to compete with the free labor of the south. So, Lincoln thought to find a way to do abolish slavery in order to create equal opportunity for all but intentionally the white workers. The declaration did not intend to include Negroes. The founders did not intend to declare all men equal in all respect. They did consider all men created equal. Equal in certain inalienable rights, among which are life liberty and the pursuit of happiness. The intention to enslave us for an eternity to free labor is appalling to imagine? But are we still slaves to the ideal of being once intended? Are we slaves to the notion of being disunited? Is this a result of our condition?

Is it the fact that we've been through so much pain – cruelty – and racism that repels us from one another? Are we now the oppressor's of our own race? Is it the tyrannical behavior that has afflicted us with great suffer the reason we continue to cause each other grief?

Do we take after the fashions of angry savages who view us with disgust? Those who assert refined decorum or propriety but showed us nothing but acts of barbarism just to extend their power of control over us? Do we wish to exert that same comportment over our own people?

I wanted to show the person before the sacrilegious image reflecting himself provided understanding of the reason his people hate each other. He doesn't see how everything that has been mentioned could cause his black brothers to destroy themselves. This can't be the reason black women are degraded. This can't be the reason we turn our backs on our brother's. This can't be the cause for their hatred towards one another. He's trying to honestly get some clarity as to why. Because the things he was informed should push his brother's and sister's closer then to divide them. Which is what the image is trying to get across in a ridiculing manner, but he doesn't get it because he is not really listening to the message.

If it's one thing that had affected us because of racism, it's the state of feeling inferior. Psychologically to this day a lot of black people still feel as if white society is better or more privileged. And that's because that state of mind has had us trapped to believe that we could never be more than the cognitive we feel is superior. We will only be as great or greater then what we think we are.

It's almost like we're immune to the conditions we once endured. We adapted in a way that made us the threat to our own wellbeing. We are now our own sickness, our own plague, and the savages that burden ourselves. We are damaged by the vulnerability of being stereotyped. Now we actually believe that we should be pursued, suspected, harassed and treated with suspicion because of the life we chose which makes us a target of police brutality or misconduct.

Still till this day, race crimes are still being committed. Black people are still being threatened, insulted, and violently attacked by the actions of simple minded people who refuse to evolve. But it's more of a shame that we are more distant from each other then we once were. There's no sincere unity. We only seem to come together after tragedy strikes. Then we are back to being strangers who wish for each other's demise.

So why should you love each other? The image that's being reflected questions his apparent self-more in a rhetorical manner. Why should black people love each other when it's clear we find excuses in everything just to hate one another. We are only adapting to the suppression that has held us back for years in this land of opportunity. Where being free is no longer a desire nor a mind state due to our miscreant ways, and the new home to where slave owners brought me to dwell in that same state whether if slavery still exist or not.

A Struggle for Silence

There's a struggle going on here!,
I said there's a struggle going on here!,

And it's happening inside as well as beyond these prison walls,

Whether we acknowledge it or not; it's a struggle that's affecting us all,

A struggle that demands we choose between opposing sides of a principled war,

Not between civilians and captives,
Or sinners and Baptist,

Nor is it about criminals or those who obey the law,

No! It's a harder choice than that; because it pertains to those who are persecuted in the same court,

Or accused in any matter deemed wrong,
It's a matter of loyalty and betrayal,

Authentic and fraudster,
Upholding the code of silence that most tend to dishonor,

Trust and deceit that alters the perception which binds those comradely,

Assured reliance which gives relief when confirmation of one's allegiance isn't breached; Upon confinement or punishment where most opt to speak because of their lack of morality,

And the shame!
Yeah, I said it; the shame of those proven to be weak when times reveal previous actions that were bleak,

Becoming a test of faith balancing the weight of the disgraced who turned state,

And the few who stand committed to their oaths to never co-operate with a system that prides it's self to see us turn on those we asseverate as an associate; wait!,

This didactic tenet isn't…..This isn't just well structured poetry,

It's a calling of integrity – strength – and confident hope to reclaim our dignity,

Disassociate yourselves ye mighty people!,
There's no dependency amongst the conduct of treachery,

To truly believe your safe guarded from the venom of a poisonous tongue makes you more foolishly then those who were betrayed by the snakes you assume are friendly,

And the audacity of you who judgement seems to be clouded,

Confused about your views when you refuse to be one that's doubted,

Accepted consequences for the violations you partake in without providing incriminating information; and got the nerve!,

Yeah; the nerve to acquaint yourselves with unworthy faces that assist in investigations or the devastation of one's liberation,

And to you who condone such traitorous characteristic's,

Compromising your standards even though your preference is contradicting,

Favoring the strong willed but express compassion for the brittle minded making the situation more conflicting,

And the impression that's given causes others to think that "telling" is an acceptable way of living,

So? I'm asking you as a people with high regards to cease using excuses for individuals who prate with loose lips; sinking relationships to avoid doing a sentence or any type of punishment due to their aid in someone's conviction,

It's a struggle going on here,

And it's sad to say that not many is taking a stand for fealty; though no one wants to be a victim of snitching.

P.O.A.P

A Struggle for Silence

THE BREAK DOWN

In this poem I wanted to address the topic of snitching. I didn't want to confront the issue in a way where those who allegedly co-operated with the law was another discussion that deserves further mindful attention. Of course, assisting in someone's conviction is something that should always receive recognition or notice, because I personally believe that treachery isn't something that should be accepted. But this is about those who remit the conduct of other's that are untrustworthy. No one likes a disloyal person in any event. There can't be favoritism in what a person chooses to condone or tolerate when it comes to dishonorable character or actions. To concede one thing but disapprove another when it comes to unscrupulous comportment is very hypocritical and bias. We as a people tend to permit deception when it's not affecting us directly or when we feel it's suitable for our own existence. But when we're the victims of such dishonor no matter the magnitude or extent we feel betrayed by those we gave our trust. I wanted to shine some light on those who pretend to despise the same thing they encourage, the same thing they continue to allow, and the thing which they comfort. The quality they wish to never experience, but the trait they welcome with open arms when they're just the observer. This is for the people who cling to the commendation of morality but are pulling towards the opprobrium of the traitorous.

I wanted to just make it known that it's a struggle going on. It's a statement that deserves everyone's attention. It's something urgent that should receive all notice and awareness. It's a struggle that demands the reader to take interest in what is going on. The second mention of a struggle is very clear that there's truly something contesting that shouldn't be ignored. People are struggling with the notion of what they should accept or disregard. Their confused about their position and where they stand on the subject of snitching. They don't know if they should condemn or support the selfish acts of others. Their struggling with the concept of something they don't approve of but continue to make exceptions for.

This struggle is happening not only within the confines of the prison system, it's happening in society as well. It's more than just a problem for those considered to be menace or uncivilized. This is an issue that should be generally recognized because anyone could be the target of betrayal. And whether we choose to be heedful or not this struggle is conflicting us all. It's affecting our judgement and views on the things we should be repelled by. It's causing a separation between those who supposed to share the same principled values. Those who are bothered or displeased with frauds and posers. It's a struggle that's confusing our belief of what's honorable and should deserve credibility, with what's indecent and immoral. It's tainting our thoughts of what we define as virtuous and praiseworthy. Whether we take notice of what's going on or continue to be bias in what we choose to accept or disregard, this struggle is really diminishing what we perceive to be noble.

This struggle demands that we pick a side and stop straddling the fence of incertitude and being undecided when it's not affecting us consequentially. We have to view each treacherous act as if it was committed against ourselves and not only pardon them when their causing someone else grief, suffering, or harm. We have to be clear in our conviction. Do we actually think it's appropriate for someone to betray another's loyalty even if that someone is us? Or do we feel that a person should accept the reality of their fate when their actions endanger their own wellbeing?

This isn't a struggle between civilians and captives. This isn't about living righteously or being a miscreant. It isn't about following the law or breaking it. It isn't about those in society or those that's incarcerated. I don't want you to view this struggle from an opposition. I want you to adhere to what's correct. This struggle isn't about sinner's and Baptist. It isn't about believers or the corrupt. Nor is it about the wickedly or the divine. It's clearly about one thing here, and that's what's right or wrong. It not just about criminals or those who obey the law. It's not just about those considered to be bad or good. It's not just about justice being served or the just being reserved. It's about the disloyalty in any event no matter what group your label to.

This struggle is about simply those who appear in the same court, on the same side of defense, in front of the same judge who's deciding their case on the same terms for their violations or misconduct. This struggle is about those who are accused in any manner or matter deemed wrong. It's about those who are prosecuted or trial for their mischief or offense. Those who are apprehended or scrutinized for their delinquent behavior. And a matter of those who doesn't see a problem with this until they're the ones who are betrayed. It's simply a matter of loyalty and dishonor. A matter of being a turn coat no matter what side of the fence you're on. No matter if you're a law-abiding citizen or a criminal. A matter of telling on the next individual who hadn't gotten caught. A matter of accepting your own responsibilities and not looking for other to share your blame. A matter of us realizing that snitching should never be condoned regardless of how we look at it. A matter of us realizing that we can't play both sides.

It's between the authentic who live up to their standards of moral conduct and those who swindle their way out of punishment because of selfish desires. It's between those who despise betrayal and the fraudsters who only feel disgusted by it when it suits them. The kind of individuals who cry foul play when they're the ones paying the price because of someone else lack of accountability but tend to proclaim nobility when their around those who aren't considered to be stand-up individuals. It's between those who pretend to uphold a code of silence but affiliate with those who don't. It's about those who act as if their trustworthy but acquaint themselves with those who can't be trusted.

Once one destroys the trust which binds a comradeship how can anyone ever think that they are capable of being reliable? How can anyone think that there can ever be fealty after that reliance has been breached? Are you that naïve to think that an individual who deceived other's that were close to him/her would honestly exempt you if it came to it? Reliability and the conscientious belief of those who conform to the pledge they make should present certainty about a person who is devoted to the oath they take. One should never have doubts about the individuals they trust in because if suspicion about dishonesty is over looked or ignored the damage that is caused by deceit could only be credited to the person who was duped and not the offender. We are responsible for our own short comings most of the time. Does it not give you comfort when you feel that you can depend on another person to have your back in times of need or worry? Does it not grant you relief when one proves to be honorable or when your faced with devastating elements and could rely on someone else to help improve or relieve you of destructive oppositions?

It's only during the time of great suffer or punishment that people opt to speak on the truths about others that would provide them comfort from those tribulation. Only then when their looking to spare themselves do they volunteer hurtful or unauthorized information because of their lack of allegiance that was never sincere. And this is truly a shame that a person can be mistrustful to someone they so called considered a friend, family, or have had any love for.

How could you expose someone else faults which wasn't being examined or suspected as the initial violation, just because you're in the spot light? How could you jeopardize someone else life or situation just to save yourself? How could you show such weak qualities when the oath you stood upon is being tested? The oath you vowed to protect?

When our loyalty is tested it proves whether we can be trusted or not. Whether our pledges are sincere. It shows a balance of our commitment and dishonor. It shows a measurement of our character and the size of our heart. It shows the proportions of our loyalty and the standard of our quality. It shows the distinction between the honorable and the disgraced. It allows us to see who we can depend on to stand firm during times of pressure or confrontation. Especially when we're suspected by a criminal system whose elation for their ostentatiously display of tactics to cause us to turn on those we earnestly assert as a partner, is something they pride themselves with. Wait! Isn't this obvious though.

I want the readers to know that although this is well structure poetry it's honestly a serious matter that should be observed. It's honestly to evaluate moral character and conduct and teach what should be ethically correct. It's a calling for us to have a code of values, to be strong through the trials we face, and to have confidence in ourselves that our devotion to one another is worth more than our selfishness. Let's reclaim our dignity.

And for those who are strong willed or has proven your worthiness, let's not continue to interact with those who aren't. Let's not continue to confuse the situation even further. Let's lead by example and spare others of such a treacherous fate. It's outrageously insane for anyone to believe that a disloyal person could be trusted because the only thing that can be relied upon in that case is treachery or deceit. And it's ridiculous for anyone to believe that a dishonorable person can be a true friend. Because true means to conform to a standard of pattern, to be consistent, and resolutely rightful. Which means their conduct would remain the same? And if you believe that your safe guarded from snakes, liars, cheaters or any kind of betrayal then your more foolish then you appear to be. Because you're only underestimating the level of their betrayal till you're the one who must witness it personally.

And the audacity of you who knows their capabilities. How could you be a victim of such dishonorable comportment and still associate yourself with those kinds of individuals? Either you don't mind being the one "thrown under the bus" as they call it or your truly so blind that your judgement is impaired by reality. You seem to be confused about your associations, but you refuse to be doubted about you being trustworthy. You'll go through heights to prove your loyalty but neglect the traits of those around you. Your adamant about accepting the individual consequences of your actions without incriminating other's but got the nerve? To friend those who would give you up at the drop of a dime.

The nerve of you to acquaint yourselves with those who assist in other's grief, other's restrictions of liberation, other's punishment, and the destruction of other's lives. But you stand on morals you say?

And to you who condone such conduct although you never been affected or lived a life of delinquency. Not knowing the circumstances of the situation but innocently supporting this treachery out of devotion to those you love or feel an obligation to. You stand by your unworthy associates with honor because that's something you claim to possess. You aid these kinds of people but when you're the victim of such deceit you then begin to hate the same thing you once assisted. How hypocritical is that? You who favor the strong willed but express compassion for the weak. You aren't sure of what's wrong or right, so you follow whatever pursues you at the time. You never stand firm on your beliefs, so you just pick and choose what to accept and what not to.

And the impression that's given from all of these different views causes people to think that snitching is an acceptable way of living.

So, I'm asking you as a people. You as trustworthy individuals. You as loyal beings with high regards for your selves. Stop using excuses for those who chatter foolishly or prate with loose lips sinking the relationships they supposed to devote themselves to, just to avoid penalties.

The last reminder was to let people know now that I may have your attention that, it's a struggle going on here that should be analyzed and taken as a very serious concern.

It's sad that many are not taking a stand for fealty. Many aren't upholding to the code of values that validates our loyalty. A lot of people are struggling with the ideal of trust and who to believe or share reliance to. Everyone is seeming to either breech their oaths of honor or is condoning those who have. It's sad because though we find it difficult to make a choice of who's credulous, no one wants to be the victim of snitching.

A Mad Life

Confusion – Confusion,
Seeing such delusion,
People thinking this world is so great; what their viewing are illusions,

Brain contusion – Brain contusion,
My mind bruised by this spurious news,
Assuming that there's any good here is just plainly foolish,

Intrusion – Intrusion,
Drugs invading the streets; guns found in the possession of minors who
haven't yet reached puberty,
Children in poverty who couldn't afford to buy their own treats,
Now waving pistols that miraculously appeared out of thin air on a
playground that was once sweet,

Who then – Who then is without sin?
No one pious to cast the first stone so the minerals are tossed from every
wicked hand,

Corruption – Corruption,
Genius influencing the weak; who tag along out of fear or manipulation
but mostly because they don't possess the quality to lead,
Insecurities impeding what they can achieve,
So, they clueless follow a path they can't see,
One that remains the past of elders they'll soon repeat,

Abduction – Abduction,

Purity snatched from the innocent by the grip of greed who seizes every desire tempted by worldly things,

Reproduction – Reproduction,
An abomination to allow same sex relation,
Adams chasing the serpent instead of pursuing the Eve's of our generation,
Deceived yet again by Satan's devilish grin; which seems veracious,
While homosexuality spreads rapidly like a disease which seems contagious,

Plantations – Plantations,
Strip clubs providing races of seductive laborers; and masculine egos who feel superior to the feminine caterers,
Women on chopping blocks disguised as stages,
Sex sells! To the highest bidder who lust for slaves of exploitation,

Obligations – Obligations,
Men whom are rivals to responsibility – fatherhood – and leadership,
Enemies to a priority that needs their parenting eagerness,
At war with a cause that deserves them to be great mentors,
But rather neglect the child of the future; whom without them often become lost,

Racist – Racism,
Still exist!,
Hate will never cease to be; Even if we all had the same color skin,

A nation – A nation,
Falling short of god's purpose for creation,
His anger increasingly infuriating with misanthrope that has been resonating from the beginning of mankind rebellious disobedience,

Harvey Howell & Shamika Gray

A mad life I say then,
A mad life we stay in,
A mad life that needs saving,
A mad life we have to change before our days end,
A mad life which is the simplest explanation.

P,O,A.P

A Mad Life

THE BREAK DOWN

Now with this poem, I just wanted to touch on a few things some people may find disturbing or questionable that's going on in today's society. I wanted to make comparisons between concerning issues that's obvious but unapparent. And I wanted to relate them to the things we find disapproving or unacceptable. I wanted to show how unbalanced this country is contrary to the things it's founded upon, the things we believe in, or the things that seems implausible to what's been proven. I wanted to show how mad this country has become. How people have come so far only to neglect what we strived to avoid. I also wanted to expose some of the things once criticized or found shameful that's now condoned. This poem is not meant to offend any reader at all. I just wanted to capture certain thoughts others may often wondered about.

I wanted to point out the confusion of all the things that are about to be said. The confusion that cause some people to feel perplexity. I wanted to make known that the notion of this world being perfect is a delusion. In order for a thing to be perfect it cannot have any flaws. And this world is full of defects. Error's that are intended to cause us to suffer but, meant to help us learn from our mistakes. Blunders and blemishes that shows us the cruel reality of our choices. It's an illusion for anyone to think that this world is so great when we strive to make it to heaven. It's almost like having a brain contusion trying to figure out why the world function the way it does or why people refuse to see it for what it is. It's honestly foolish of them to believe that there's any good here other then what could be achieved through the purpose of worship.

I wanted to bring awareness about the fact that drugs and guns continue to invade inner city neighborhoods. And ending up in the possession of young children who can't even afford to provide for themselves. How is it that these young children who are in poverty, that has barely reached puberty, could obtain government issue hand guns or unlicensed hand guns without any identification? Children that are all of a sudden waving pistols at each other. I wanted to show the innocents of these children, who in one minute went from playing in parks or play grounds to killing each other for nothing.

I wanted to state that no one is pious. No one is incapable of error. We could never be perfectly fit for a position to judge other's even if we qualify. So, the stones of reproof are often thrown from every wicked hand we allow such power to. The power that can determine our fate or decide our path.

It's known that there are strong individuals who are worthy of being leaders. And there are weak individuals who is better suited to follow. But although you may have that weak quality, it doesn't mean that you should allow yourself to be led to your destruction because of anyone else. And when I speak of strong, it's mostly in a sense of being strong minded or intellectually stable. And having an effect on the weaker minds who can't really think for themselves because of their insecurities of temporary defeat or failure. I'm also talking about the young people who are being misguided by the older crowd who feel they can lead due to their experience. Those who are persuaded by the influence of those before them who chose to lead them astray as well-being that their lives weren't successful. Or because they never found the need to change that which has been unproductive.

In this poem I wanted to make the comparison between abduction and the innocent lives taken away from a person because of their greed. Now we all know the word abduction means to kidnap or take by force. And the time during a person's life when they're considered to be the most innocent is when their a child. But I wanted the reader to understand that the innocents that's taken away is not an actual child but the purity of a person before their corrupted by the greed of having worldly things.

Now this sequence may be a little offensive to many although it's not my attention to attack anyone. I just wanted to address a touchy topic that most find acceptable these days. America is supposed to stand on the religion of Christianity. In the bible it speaks of sodomy and same sexual relations. It spoken of being an abomination to indulge in such acts. Adams of our times chasing the serpent, which is an interest of deception, instead of pursuing the Eve's that God had chosen for us. Now I'm going off what's been legislated according to the bible. I wanted to show Satan's craftiness and the promise he made to lead mankind astray. And show that the grounds this country stands on religiously are contradicting and unstable. I don't have anything against homosexuality. I think a person business is their own and we will be judged for our individual acts of conduct. It's just something that seems to be forcing its self on society by becoming a part of every social functioning. In the United States of America same sex marriages has been legalized nationwide since June 26, 2015. When the United States Supreme Court ruled in Obergefell v. Hodeges that state-level bans on same sex marriages are unconstitutional, the Courts ruled that the denial of marriage licenses to same sex couples and the refusal to recognize those marriages performed in other jurisdictions violates the due process and the equal protection clauses of the Fourteenth Amendment of the United States Constitution. The ruling overturned a precedent, Baker v. Nelson. While Civil Rights campaigning took place from the 1970's, the issue became prominent from around 1993 when the Hawaii Supreme Court ruled in Baehr v. Lewin, that the prohibition was unconstitutional. The ruling led to federal action and actions by several states, to restrict marriage to male or female couples, in particular the Defense of Marriage Art (DOMA).

During the period of 2003 to 2015 various lower court decisions, state legislation and popular referendums had already legalized same sex marriages to some degree in thirty eight out of fifty U.S. States. In the U.S. territory Guam, and in the District of Columbia. In 2013 the Supreme Court overturned a key provision of DOMA, declaring part of it unconstitutional and in breach of the Fifth Amendment in United States v. Windsor because it singled out a class of person for discrimination by refusing to treat their marriages equally under federal law when state laws had created them equally valid.

The ruling led to the federal government's recognition of same sex marriages, with federal benefits for married couples connected to either the state of residence or the state in which the marriage was solemnized. However, the ruling focused on provision of DOMA responsible for the federal government refusing to acknowledge state sanctioned same sex marriages leaving the question of state marriages laws itself to the individual states. The Supreme Court addressed that question two years later in 2015 ruling in Obergefell, that same sex married couples were to be constitutionally accorded the same recognition as opposite sex couples as state/territory levels as well as at federal level. By the time that same sex marriage became legal nationally public opinion on the subject had reached almost 60% approval levels according to polls by The Wall Street Journal, the Human Rights Campaign, and CNN having been consistently over 50% since 2010 and trending consistently upward over the years prior.

Now a day's homosexuality is considered a norm. Some people still frown upon the act that God has forbidden us from. But society has found a way to make it acceptable all across America.

It's apparent that strip clubs are one of the greatest attractions these days. And that women no longer feel shameful about shedding their clothes for money or exposing their bodies which supposed to be revealed only for the eyes of their husbands. They don't feel regretful or disgraced to indulge in sexual acts just to provide for themselves or their kids. To me, the strip clubs became the new plantation where the stage is identical to the chopping blocks during early slavery. Slaves were brought to America by ships. When they were put onto the ships, they were stripped naked and shacked two by two. Slave auctions were held in the South and the North before the American Civil War. Before selling the slaves, a captain did everything he could to improve the price he would get for them. The women were exploited, humiliated and often stripped nude to appeal to the interest of paying slave owners and to show how healthy they were due to the conditions they suffered because of the ships. The slave was always disparaging and defamed at every chance to show that they weren't human beings or that they weren't civilized creatures. Slave families often were separated and sold to slave holders in distant states. Back in those times they use to produce the Africans who were considered cattle on chopping blocks to the highest bidders to be enslaved. Exactly like what's going on now except, for them being enslaved. Women are placed on stages where dollar bills are tossed at them as they engage in all kinds of indecencies. Losing their integrity and morality. Slaves were bought for various amounts which is nothing in true value for the possession of a person. And women are now being bought with dollars to defile what would be respectfully sacred. These days strippers have no shame about their actions, nor do they have any regards of the way their debased.

I couldn't help but to address the lack of father figures out there. It's a major crisis that needs to be acknowledged on a level of urgent reform. There are a lot of issues that the world is adamant about changing. But I don't think that fatherhood is as much of a focal attention that it should be. It seems like men are rivals to the responsibility they help create. An obligation that's abandoned without care. An enemy to a priority that should be their main concern. There are not just children forsaken by desertion. They are kids who are shareholders of the future and robbed of a chance to have the right guidance in their lives. Policy makers at last are coming to recognize the connection between the breakdown of American families and various social problems. Children born into single parent families are much more likely than children of intact families, to fall into poverty and welfare dependence themselves in later years. Those children in fact, face a daunting array of problems. While the link between illegitimacy and chronic welfare dependency is now becoming better understood, we also need to appreciate another strong and disturbing pattern evident in scholarly studies. The link between illegitimacy and violent crime and between the parent attachments and violent crime. Without an understanding of the root causes of criminal behavior how criminals are formed members of congress and state legislators cannot understand why whole sectors of society particularly in urban areas, are being torn apart by crime. A review of the empirical evidence in the professional literature of the social sciences gives us an insight into the root causes of crime. Consider for instance over the past 30 years, the rise in violent crime parallels the rise in families abandoned by father's. High crime neighborhoods are characterized by high concentration of families abandoned by fathers. State by State analysis by heritage scholars indicate that a 10 percent increase in the percentage of children living in single parent homes lead typically to a 17 percent increase in juvenile crime. The rate of violent teen crime corresponds with the number of families abandoned by fathers. The types of aggression and hostility demonstrated by a future criminal often is for shadowed in unusual aggressiveness as early as age 5 or 6 years old. The future criminal tends to be an individual rejected by other children as early as the 1st grade who goes on to form his own group of friends, often the future delinquent gang. Well over 90% of children from safe stable homes do not become delinquents. By contrast, only 10% of children from unsafe and unstable homes in these neighborhoods avoid crime. The father's authority and involvement in raising his child are also a great buffer against a life of crime. The scholarly evidence in short, suggest that the heart of the explosion of crime in America is the loss of the capacity of father's and mother's to be responsible in caring for the child they bring into the world. This loss of love and guidance at the intimate levels of family has broad social consequence for the children and for the wider community. The empirical evidence shows that too many young men and women from broken homes tend to have a much weaker sense of connection with their neighborhood and are prone to exploit its member to satisfy their unmet needs or desires.

We must be better fathers to our children and more involved as parents. The lust or love that help creates a child shouldn't be the thing that drives a person away if the companionship doesn't work. There's still an obligation to be that child father. There's still an obligation to help set a better path for the future of our children.

Once largely limited to poor women and minorities, single motherhood is now becoming the new norm. this prevalence is due in part to the growing trend of children born outside of marriage. A societal trend that was virtually unheard-of decades ago. About 4 out of 10 children were born to unwed mothers. Nearly two-thirds are born to mothers under the age of 30. Of all single parent families in the U.S. single mothers make up the majority. According to U.S. Census Bureau, out of about 12 million single parent families in 2014, more than 80% were headed by single mothers. Today 1 in every 4 children under the age of 18 a total of about 17 million being raised without a father and nearly half 45% live below the poverty line.

For those living with father's only about 21% live in poverty. In contrast, among children living with both parents only 13% are counted as poor. The statistics of single parent families are 83% single mother families which is 9,929,000. And for single father's is 17% which is 1,945,000.

This was something that became an annoyance to me. From time to time I would hear people say that racism no longer exist. I didn't want to get to deep into what is obvious, but I wanted to make known that as much as there is hate racism will never cease to be even if we were all alike in every way. For example, there's Black on Black crime just as there is White on White crime. Murders hadn't just begun to happen. Cain and Abel were the first act of violence or taking of a person's life out of envy and hatred. And they were brothers. So how can one think that hatred doesn't reside in others who feel that this country belongs solely to them, and that Black people have no share. And looking at a lot of the discrimination that continues to take place only validate that racism still exist.

This is a nation falling short of what God intended as our purpose due to the fact that it's following that same destructive path of every town, city, or nation that was destroyed in the Bible. Since Adam, we were doomed as a people but given a chance to prove ourselves worthy as a devout servant. Our rebellion and disobedience continue to only raise the question if our creation was a good ideal as the angels once questioned. The expression of a mad life is recognized here concerning the reality of things, the way we live, the change we need to make, the actions we need to take before the end of our lives as to father's, and the only way to concisely explain it.

Judged as a Jezebel pt. 2

Look at you with your independent stride and professional demeanor,

Your sophisticated look and educated potential that's eager,

Your decent mannerism and proper comportment; and your public display of correct decorum,

What a treasure to see your achievements from driven pursuit; but still your judged by what you do in privacy as if that defines you,

Your demand for respect and equality; When most denied you to do what you do,

Your stance for social change due to your neglectful role in society; in which your fight was proof,

Your business sense that's a perfect stitch like the threads in your business suite,

And your effectiveness to lead; showing true quality that wasn't viewed,

But still your perceived for personal things as if your only acknowledged by what eludes,

Your strength and endurance to surmount difficulty-adversity-and hardship,

Your commitment to stay driven despite tension-affliction-or torment,

The trials that's catastrophic and deterrent which proves your ambition to be apparent,

Your natural acceptance of accountability and responsibility as a parent,

And your ability to manage your career and motherhood without being stagnant,

But it seems your mostly observed for your personal satisfaction,

Your devotion through the treachery; and commitment through the madness,

The sacrifice performed respectfully; and the adherence you establish,

Your partnership in love; and the pleasure received with passion,

Yet your seen like a nymph because you just wish to preserve your marriage,

The beautiful Jezeble.

P.O.A.P

Judged as a Jezebel PT.2

PT.2

THE EXPLANATION

This poem is a dedication to women of all nationalities and qualifications. It's a contribute to the striving, independent, activist, single women (who are parents or not), and married women who are criticized for their sexuality. Women who are labelled with demeaning names that offensively insults their integrity I wanted to give an explanation to this poem being that It's mostly about the glorification of women rather than their sexuality. Instead of commenting on what society object to or find disgraceful. I wanted to point out what should, more so, receive our focused. The things that deserves our acknowledgement and is done for the purpose of general attention. And not the private matters that should be disregarded. I wanted to show the success of women and some of their substantial body of work. The things they've done or assisted us with, in making this country remarkable. We as a society have a tendency to undervalue the service devoted by Women, and stereotype them in general, because of their lustful desires. We've categorized them into one class when defining women by their sexual relations or how they conduct themselves with their personal affairs. And I wanted to show a distinction between a woman of value and one who actions is considered to be opprobrious.

The lines in this poem mention the types of women who are independent and professional due to their demeanor or stride which is a reference to the self-sufficient women who doesn't feel the need to rely on anyone else for any support or financial help. The demand for social change is a reference to the women activist who stood for equality and fought for women's liberation. The business sense that's a perfect stitch represents the business women who business suit is well structured just as she is. The strength and endurance through the trials that's catastrophic and deterrent is a reference to the striving women who continue to be determined. The responsible woman who is accountable is the single mom managing her career and raising her children, that has stayed strong through difficulty, adversity, hardship, and still provides a life for her progeny. The committed women who makes sacrifices in love and devoted herself even after the treachery, the loyal or married women who is willing to please and pleasure her man by any means. Each description illustrates the importance of women in every aspect. Women who are likened to immoral females and are condemned for engaging in certain urges without committing themselves to one steady individual. Although their actions are not done maliciously or intentionally to cause separation. Shouldn't they be given more credit than that of a loose women or tramp? Shouldn't they be viewed with more respect than what we define as a hoe, slut, or a jezebel? Should there be a standard as to what qualify the behavior of our women as shameful or disgracing? Because if not then how could we determine the jezebel.

Judged as A Jezebel PT.2

THE BREAK DOWN

In this poem judged as a jezebel, I wanted to focus more on the accomplishments women have achieved throughout the years instead of their promiscuous desires to be unrestrained. I wanted to point out all the things that seem to escape our notice when viewing the worth of women. They are judged by their personal preference rather than their general contribution. And perceived with disparaging epithets or negative stereotypes in the most discerning manner. Society always found a way to discredit women and hinder their ability to flourish. Even if their work ethics in a professional setting is outstanding, women are still undervalued or overlooked. I wanted to acknowledge everything women have stood for in this poem while addressing the issue of them being labelled as a jezebel. Another despoiling title that defame women. I wanted to show their strength, will, and capability. And mention the things that society refuse take heed to or ignore when women do not conform to its standards.

I decided to start with an ideal that would be a representation for independent women by describing the way she proudly walks. A lot of women who has that independent mind frame usually have a high level confidence because they appear to have everything going for themselves. They sort of feel self-sufficient when it comes to being financially established. They've seemed to have acquired a comfortable life for themselves on their own. And they're normally sophisticated and very educated in their field or work. An independent woman is very driven, persistent, and professional at what she does. And she also carries herself with dignity and respect. Sometimes the life of an independent woman, just as any hard-working man, doesn't allow them the leisure time to attend to their personal life due to their ambitious desire to succeed. Sometimes their dedication to their work career prevents them from finding a stable companion to settle down with. In which they may enjoy a little transitory pleasure from time to time to fulfill their urging needs. Some people may argue that if women would settle for the traditional roles they would have more time to find them a great man whom they could commit to. And not randomly engage in sex occasionally with one or multiple partners. But why should they have to make that kind of sacrifice just to have a steady companionship? Why should they have to stagnate themselves just to settle down. When it comes to hardworking man who isn't married or has a consistent relationship, those same standards aren't expected of them. Men aren't held to the same expectancy of a women and is exceptionally given amnesty in most cases. But when it comes to women, they are governed with much more regulations then men. They are viewed through a scolding scope and judged with the harshest rulings. They are thought to be rubbish and defiled when they do something outside of those regulated guidelines. And are considered to be trifling when their personal or feminine nature is being questioned. With all that women have strived diligently to accumulate, how could our perception of them be so easily tainted by the actions or distinctions that shouldn't be of any concern to us, nor an issue of acknowledgement compared to the accomplishments they have achieved.

Women fight for Equality is truly a monument of history. They've stood for social change at a time when men had dominated every essential field of work. Women generally had fewer legal rights and career opportunities than men. They have always been discriminated against when it comes to what their purpose would be. Wifehood and motherhood were regarded as women's most significant professions. They weren't allowed to have a voice in earlier times and had to fight to be heard as well as share a place amongst men, which was never easy and still isn't. Throughout time, most societies have held women in an inferior status compared to that of men. It's often justified as being the natural result of biological difference between sexes because they are figured to be less powerful, less decisive, more emotional, or smaller. These conceptions over the period of time led to the women's movement for social change during the 1800's. Leading women thinkers began to emphasize the rights of individuals. Business, political, professional, and religion have been traditionally dominated by men. The thinkers in the Age of Reason, questioned the establishment of political and religious authority and stressed the importance of reason, equality, and liberty. Fundamental changes took root as a new intellectual atmosphere helped justify women's rights to full citizenship. On the eve of the French Revolution (1789-1799), the Marguis De Condorcet, a French philosopher, spoke in favor of women's right to vote. In the American Colonies, the Revolutionary War (1775-1783), fought in the name of liberty and equality, women supported the war with their sewing and farming, and by boycotting British goods and engaging in other forms of protest. But Americans nor the French revolutions increased women's rights at the time.

The spread of industrialization during the 1800's also affected women. The Industrial Revolution moved men's, women's and children's work out of the home and into the factories. Factory jobs offered working-class women an opportunity to earn wages but if they were married, their husbands legally controlled their earnings.

In the beginning of the women's movement, women began to form many kinds of groups based on common interest after the French Revolution. In the United States and Britain, two major types of women's movement gradually developed. "Social", or "domestic", women's movements and "equal rights" feminist groups. Women's social movements carried out religious, charitable, and social activities. Equal rights feminist primarily worked to remove educational and political barriers on women and to change the role of women. Women have fought continuously to either be recognized, considered, or viewed equally as men for their efforts and contribution. During the 1840's and 1850's many states enacted property laws such as allowing married women to make contracts, to own property and control their earnings, to have joint custody of their children, voting, birth control issues, and better jobs and positioning. In which they weren't deemed fit or suited at first to control on their own, because they were women. In 1848, New York gave married women the right to retain control of their own real estate and personal property. The new laws especially aided widowed, deserted, and mistreated wives. The Women's Rights convention adopted a Declaration of Sentiments which called for women to receive "all the rights and privileges which belong to them as citizens of the United States". Women weren't just active in the fight for their equality. Many of the equal rights feminists were also leaders in the movement to abolish slavery. During the Civil War most women reformers devoted their efforts to supporting war activities.

In 1960 informal women's liberation groups, which were formed by female students active in the civil rights movement and in radical political organizations. There groups emphasized self-awareness and open discussion to combat discrimination and established greater equality between men and women in marriage, child-rearing, education, and employment. President John F. Kennedy's Commission on the Status of Women, founded in 1961, discovered a number of legal barriers to women's equality. It reported on the laws that barred women from jury service, excluded women from certain occupations, and in general, kept women from enjoying their full rights as citizens. In 1966, a number of feminist leaders formed the National Organization for Women (NOW) to fight sexual discrimination. The Women's Equity Action League, founded in 1968, monitored educational programs to detect inequalities in faculty pay and promotion. The organization drew attention to what was called the "chilly classroom climate", an environment that discouraged discussion participation by female students. The National Women's Political caucus, formed in 1971, focused on finding and supporting women candidates for political office. Title VII of the Civil Rights Act passed, prohibiting job discrimination on the basis of sex, color, race, national origin, and religion. And the Equal Pay Act also passed requiring equal pay for men and women doing the same work. Title IX of the Education Amendments of 1972 bans discrimination on the basis sex by schools and colleges receiving federal funds. The law has applied to discrimination in all areas of school activities, including admissions, athletics, and educational programs. The Equal Credit Opportunity Act took effect in 1975. It prohibited banks, stores, and other organizations from discriminating on the basis of sex or marital status in making loans or granting credit.

In the 20th century, as participation by women in government, the professions, and the military had increased dramatically the number of organizations formed by women has grown accordingly. Contemporary women's movement have changed may people's views about male and female roles. These changes have affected the workplace, the family, and the way women live their lives. The intellectual business sense of a women has been extremely resourceful in the furtherance of major companies. Though a notable difference in outlook still exist between the sexes. And the final outcome of these changing attitudes and values has yet to be seen. But it appears that the blurring distinctions between the roles and the trend towards greater equality of the sexes of both genders continues to be an issue our women face.

Till this day society still refuse to give women their due acceptance for all they've strived for, for all they've overcame, and for all they've achieved. Women have proved their strengths and endurance with their calls for equality, and they've continued to prove their toughness by keeping the family cohesive and maintaining work and motherhood when they are forced to juggle both. Or standing by their companions through the ups and downs. And supporting us men through our shortcomings, misfortune, and anguishes. Women have been devoted to men through our treachery and betrayal even when our actions are extremely devastating at times. They've stayed loyal through conflicting circumstances that is discouraging. And have sacrificed a great deal of their patience, energy, and lives for us. But we as men, haven't sacrificed as much or been as supportive of them and their desire to be viewed with equal opportunity, equivalent status, and parallel remuneration. And to judge them without sexism or inferiority. When they've been just as dedicated to our cause and purpose throughout history as their own. We always find a way to diminish their value whether it's denying their rights or degrading them by use of foul names just to show our superiority or to make them feel worthless. As long as a woman isn't interposing on another's relationship or causing any harm, division, or gloom to anyone else while engaging in her sexual pursuits, it shouldn't cause offense to anybody or subject women to be labelled. Let's stop the discrimination against our women as well as the defamation of those who are not deserving of such insult. We should love our sister's instead of causing them to suffer.

Ferguson

Burn down Ferguson heard by protestors enraged by the verdict of a justice systems injustice for a black race,

A woman cries out in pain; whom shrieks sound throughout a nation affected by her screams,

Outraged by the events that has took place she yells "they're a damn lie", before breaking down into sobs due to her son's killer not being charged or indicted for using excessive force on the job,

Burn this Bitch down!

Consoled by her husband who then expresses raw emotions because another police officer is pardon from persecution for the murder of an innocent black teen he claims made him feel like a five-year-old to hulk Hogan,

Burn this Bitch down!

An inconceivable notion and bazaar comparison in case you haven't noticed the six foot two inches; two-hundred-and-ten-pound officer compare to Mike Browns six foot five; two-hundred-and-eighty-pound alleged victim and culprit,

Burn this Bitch down!

How could one even assimilate something so bogus when it's hard to imagine such a theory when both persons doesn't differ that much in size,

But I guess the difference lies in the complexion of the skin if you seriously focus,

Burn this Bitch down!

Damage control could be cogent and extremely persuasive when it comes to races but only if the victim isn't Caucasian then you'll realize the system's omnipotence,

Burn this Bitch down!

Justification of slayings corroded by the recurring of black lives taken and the only consequence is demotion or relieve of duty in some cases just to ease commotion,

Burn this Bitch down!

None penalized for their crimes of hatred as long as they procure a badge that makes it legal for their ruthless motives which exempts them from being roguish,

Wait! Burn this Bitch down!

Shot six times? Now tell me who seem more possessed or demonized?

With hands held high the decision shouldn't be a difficult surmise,

And still; what expression do one expect to see in the eyes of a person who fear they may die?,

Burn this Bitch down!

The same remorseless expression officer Gary Wilson depicted in an interview when he confided that he was satisfied with the way things transpired,

Or was he satisfied that he got away with taking a young black male's life in which his unpunished conduct didn't affect him enough to sympathize,

Or to feel humanized,

Or to empathize with a parent who's been traumatized; and mortified by the results of a grand jury that left her feeling devitalized,

Burn this Bitch Down!

So many inquisitions that reside,

And where was the prosecutor? Was a question on everyone's mind,

Did he even show up at the grand jury proceeding in Mike Brown's defense?

Or did he forget he was legal representation for the opposite side he failed to represent?

Burn this Bitch down!

No cross examination; not even a witness brought forth in the case to counter the defense,

What happened to those who gave earlier statements of the incident which was broad cast on news stations?

Is it that difficult to get some one's testimony in a court room especially when they've already gave their account publicly of escalated events?

Tell me does any of this makes sense?

Slogans on t-shirts and picket signs as well as chanted by protesters who aren't convinced,

Black lives matter and our contribution to this country should be evident,

But if there's no justice how can there be peace when we're continuously slaughtered and not granted the equal rights which permits those in grief,

Burn this Bitch down!

Business and automobiles subverted by those inflamed; as looters and vandalism exploit this opportunity just to simply destroy things or possess whatever they can obtain,

Owner's devastated by the aftermath of the destruction while other's trying to make sense of what remain,

Truly a shame but some actions can't be explained when driven by pain,

Even the conduct of those who target the wrong source for their loss – misfortune – or strain,

And though what happened wasn't right; It was the one who antagonized these hostile comportments deserving blame,

Because the cost hurts all when vengeance is sort to gain,

Hands up don't shoot yet another black teen is slain,

So it's said.....Burn this Bitch down! And apologies to the people who didn't deserve to be caught in the flames.

P.O.A.P

Ferguson

THE BREAK DOWN

The shooting of Michael "mike" Brown that happened on August 9, 2014 is what sparked the Ferguson Missouri protest, looting, and arsons. Brown an 18-year-old African American male, was fatally shot by Darren Wilson a 28-year white Ferguson police officer. Shortly before the shooting Brown allegedly stole several packages of cigarillos from a nearby convenience store and shoved the store clerk. Brown was accompanied by his friend Dorian Johnson. Officer Wilson had been notified by the dispatch of the robbery and provided descriptions of two suspects. He encountered Brown and Johnson as they were walking down the middle of the street. Wilson said that he realized that the two men matched the robbery suspects descriptions. Wilson blocked the two individuals off with his cruiser and an altercation ensued with Michael Brown and the officer. A brief struggle occurred with Mike and the officer through the window of the cruiser. The officer reached for his gun to gain control of the situation in which Mike Brown fled along with his friend and the officer in pursuit. The officer exits his vehicle with his gun drawn on Mike Brown who had then stopped fleeing and turns to face the officer with his hands held up in surrender. As Brown moved towards the officer with his hands up, the officer begins to fire his weapon striking Mike Brown in the arm and other areas of this body. In the entire altercation twelve shots were fired including the fatal shot to the head of Mike Brown.

The shooting sparked unrest in Ferguson. The hands up don't shoot account was widely circulated within the black community immediately.

Harvey Howell & Shamika Gray

It contributed to the strong protestation and outrage about the killing of the unarmed young man. Protest both peaceful and violent, along with vandalism and looting contrived for more than a week in Ferguson. Police established a nightly curfew. The response of area police agencies in dealing with the protest was strongly criticized by the media and politicians. There were concerns over insensitivity, tactics, and a militarized response. Missouri Governor Jay Nixon ordered local police organizations to cede much of their authority to the Missouri State Highway Patrol.

A grand jury was called and given extensive evidence from Robert McCulloch, the St. Louis County prosecutor, in a highly unusual process on November 24, 2014. McCulloch announced that the St. Louis County grand jury had decided not to indict Wilson. On March 4, 2015 the U.S. Department of Justice reported the conclusion of its own investigation and cleared Wilson of Civil rights violations in the shooting also. It found that witnesses who corroborated the officer's account were credible, and it was also supported by forensic evidence.

Now in this case I wanted to know how could evidence support the officer's claim if Michael Brown was shot in the arms while in a surrendering position? How could it be self-defense for the officer who shot this young man twelve times in the upper body area? Are police trained to kill offenders or bring them to justice? If Mike Brown wouldn't resist moving toward the officer couldn't he have just shot him in the legs once or so to prevent him from attacking, if that was the motive?

I want to know what tactics are these police officer's trained to apply when they encounter a miscreant? Is their duty or agenda to kill if they encounter any resistance? Is their job to serve the public only if they're not in violation of the law and neglect the welfare of those who are offenders? What's the point of having a court system if police are allowed to hold court in the streets? Americans grapple with the trust between minority communities and law enforcement after a series of deaths of unarmed black men at the hands of police. There have been many incidents that have generated vigorous debate about the relationship of law enforcement and African Americans. And police use of force doctrine in Missouri and nationwide. There's a long list of police brutality and excessive conduct which resulted in the deaths of many African Americans dating back to slavery and the reconstruction era. I would like to take this time to remember a few black people that have been killed unjustly by authorized figures this same year.

Eric Gardner of Staten Island, New York.
Michael Gray of Baltimore.
Walter Lamer Scott of North Charleston, South Carolina
Earnest Satterwhite of Edgefield, South Carolina
Tony Robinson of Madison, Wisconsin
Eric Harris of Tulsa, Oklahoma
Brandon Glenn of Venice, California
Jeremy Lett of Tallahassee, Florida
And
Thomas Allen of Wellston, Missouri

There were countless of unjustly deaths that occurred in the year of 2015 by authoritative figures. More than I would have liked to report unfortunately due to my lack of resources and unfavorable circumstances.

The only way to change this outcome is to change the way the system train it's officers to address the approach of a problem. The officer's safety is always important, but a civilian life is also significant regardless if they've violated the law or is suspected of doing any wrong.

Ferguson

THE SITUATION

In this poem, I just wanted to dedicate something to the Ferguson incident that took place. I was also one of the people emotionally disturbed and affected by the tragic events that took place with everything concerning the Ferguson situation. And just needed to vent. But I wanted to speak on the factual things that took place. I wanted to address every issue while relating the exact proceedings through my poetic expressions. Some of the issues pertain to racism and discrimination. But my views or opinions are never to offend anyone or anybody of people. It's only to give my perspective and shine a light on what's apparent.

I wanted to just show the one thing that stood out before things became chaotic. I wanted to point out the phrase that started all the protestation and malicious intents caused by the injury and insults of provoked emotions. I wanted to start from the initial upset and disappointment, while taking readers through all the accounts because of the verdict which sparked the phrase "Burn this Bitch down!". Is what incited the sad turn of events. I also wanted to make mention how unfair to the Black race the justice system truly is. And to make aware that it's not only these tragedies that shows and unbalance scale in our courts.

In this poem I wanted to show a mother's pain. The pain of losing her first child. The pain she had to experience a second time after hearing the verdict. The pain the entire nation felt right before the phrase had been yelled. I wanted to show what should have been the focus of things. A woman hurting for her child lost twice. One being his life and the other being the justice she didn't receive.

I wanted people to identify with her hurt again. I wanted them to see her and the family's irrational state. I wanted them to imagine going through what she had to endure, and picture themselves for a moment losing faith in our justice system. A system that they would have never figured to be that unjust or uncompassionate. How could we justify a killing by authority with excessive force? Excessive force should be described when severely assaulting a person more than necessary but, it should never result in anyone losing their life. It should be a clear matter to determine that excessive force is not what you call this. A life was taken in a manner that is brutal. A young man was shot down like an animal who couldn't be stopped. Is that how Black people are viewed.

The chants of burn this bitch down all through the poem is an expression to show or make a point about something evident. I wanted to try to give reader's a visual of the mom and step dad that day outside the court house awaiting the verdict that devastated them both. A judgement that caused her to shriek so loud that the world heard her cries. When I came across this story on the news I was completely shocked but, more surprised that the media were blaming Mike Browns step father for igniting the burning and destruction of Ferguson county. I just couldn't believe that they were actually faulting one man for the actions of other people who were tired of being treated as if their lives didn't matter. Anyone could honestly tell there was something more which provoked the inexcusable conduct that was displayed. Indeed, a voice is powerful but, it has to already be a broader reason for justification or a burning desire to act on things that are incentive. Like the fact that police officers continue to be let off the hook for the murders of black children. Or the fact that no justice is being received. The legal system is very discriminatory when it comes to Black people. From the way we're arrested, up to the persecutions. We are far more targeted and mistreated than any other race which is a known fact.

When it comes to the court system, the prosecutors are the ones who are responsible for seeking a conviction. It's their duty to serve the courts as well as the victim(s) in a case, and to make sure that the violation that was committed is disciplined. Prosecutors often exert their discretion to the highest level of regulations with in their authority. It's their code of ethics to put loyalty to the highest moral principle and to country above loyalty to persons, party, or Government department. It's their obligation to uphold the constitution, laws, and legal regulations of the United States and all governments therein and never be a party to their evasion. They are prohibited discriminating unfairly by the dispense of special favors or privileges to anyone, whether for remuneration or not; and never accept for himself or his family, favors or benefits under circumstances which might be construed by reasonable persons as influencing the performance of his governmental duties. And it seems they do their jobs to the fullest when a person of color is on the defense. So how was it possible that they didn't even bother to present a suitable case in this incident? Was it because of the favor of the officer being someone of the law, or was it a favor of him being white? And I made it my intention to point out the comparison that officer Gary Wilson made about his size and height. He claimed that the young man made him feel like a child versus Hulk Hogan. It was a comparison made during an interview on 60 minutes or one of the shows on CNN. I can't honestly remember which one but, when I heard it I kept feeling empathy for the parents. I was honestly enraged at the liken. I wanted to have people actually analyze this comment and see how bogus it sounds. How upsetting and disappointing it could be to hear someone make such a foolish allegory. How could anyone make that kind of analogy with someone almost their size and weight? It's impossible to comprehend such a thing when a child is more than 200 or more pounds less than Hulk and probably 10 or more feet shorter than the Hulk. Now this is just an estimated guess but, in what way could that ever be considered coming from a person who is only three inches shorter and 70 pounds lighter? I guess the true comparison lies in the complexion of Mike Brown's skin than anything else. But everything that was mentioned only stirred focus away from the important question, was Mike Brown the aggressor? And even if he was, should it have cost him his life?

Now I want to make a bold statement. I want to point out the fact that if it were a white child who suffered such a tragedy, there wouldn't have been an acquittal. We probably wouldn't even be having this discussion. When it comes to law enforcement or other law agencies, I truly believe that they'll do anything to cover up their wrong to avoid any back lash. And the excuses that are presented could be extremely persuasive when it comes to black and white issues. But I don't think that a matter as the shooting of a white person, who is presumed to be a threat or "the aggressor" if the only danger is resisting arrest, would be quickly resolved without any authorized figure being tried or penalized for the life that was taking. It seriously makes black people wonder if Americans feel their lives truly matter. This wasn't the only case in 2015 where a young Black teen life was taken by officers of the law. But there was way more acquittals or justifications for why their lives were taken then there were officers being held accountable for their actions. How did these killings continue to recur without any changes to police conduct being made? How could these young Black teens continue to be slaughtered and the only consequence that were given out was demotion or relief of duty. Only law suits seem to guarantee more of a satisfying ruling than receiving justice, as if these children lives are only meant to be compensated with a civil suit. Like their families could rest easily knowing that even though they lost a child they no longer have any money issues.

I couldn't help but to insert into this poem that these police officers feel that as long as they wear a badge that they're above the law. It's almost as if the badge they wear justify their behavior instead of rectifying it. It makes it acceptable and inculpable for them to kill these children in a manner that's alarming. The entire country had taken notice and Black mothers were fearful for their kids leaving their homes without ending up gunned down by some quick trigger police officer. But the scariest part about this all is that most of the teenagers who were killed weren't thugs, gang-banger, or criminally affiliated. The reality that even if their kids were on the right path could still subject parents to such a tragedy is very frightening. They were innocent kids who probably were only misbehaving at the time of their deaths but, still it doesn't give the authority the right to play judge. It wasn't just inner-city kids who were being targeted or threatened by this awareness. It was Black families everywhere. City kids were only suffering from this kind of brutality all their lives. But the main issue apart from those who are suffering is the fact that being an officer exempt a person from being roguish when he's still human and liable to make bad judgement calls. That's honestly the scariest thing of them all when one considers that reason for their suffering.

Mike Brown was shot six times by a professionally trained officer who is supposedly competent in the matter of defusing or deescalating a situation. So why was there a need to shoot this teen six times in the upper torso of his body? Couldn't this officer used other precautions or simply just aimed for the legs if his intentions were only to desist and restrain this young man. Couldn't this officer had applied other methods to detain Mike Brown or prevent his life from being taken? Did he even consider any other tactics? I mean could he have done anything else to control the situation other than shooting the teenager in the upper body area or the head? In his interview, the officer had claimed that the teenager seemed possessed or demonized. How is a person expected to act when they're frightened or shot? How should a person react when their life is threatened or they're in fear of dying? Of course, they might seem possessed to the one who is trying to take their life. And with Mike Browns hands held high in a state of surrender how could he be viewed as being demonic? When a person holds up their hands to surrender it's a form of submission not aggression. It's clear that Mike Brown was giving up and complying with the officer who he felt endangered by. And that shouldn't be too difficult to surmise due to what's mentioned. And even if that was the case of his expression which could have been fear that cause him to have an unusual drive or effectiveness, doesn't mean that his intentions were to danger the officer. It could be that he was trying to avoid his life being taken. And if expressions were truly something to watch or weigh in on the matter. In the interview with officer Gary Wilson, he confided that he was satisfied with the way things turned out with him and the teenager. There was this proud and chilling demeanor about officer Gary when he said this as if he had got away with something horrific. There was no remorse for the family or for the simple fact that Mike Brown was just a child. There was no consideration for his family's lost or the pain a parent would suffer from losing their child.

I wanted to pose the question, was he honestly satisfied that he was still alive or that he accomplished what he intended? This was more of a questioning of reason. Was officer Gary satisfied that he got away with taking this young Black males' life because he wasn't punished for it? And was it because he wasn't affected by any repercussions that it didn't affect him enough to sympathize with the teenager's family? Would it have been different if his freedom was at stake? Would it have affected him enough to feel humanized then? I mean in any event, it's the humanity of a person to feel regretful for the tragic loss of another person even if it was in the nature of self-defense. And officer Gary Wilson didn't empathize even as a human being. But why not? How come there was no emotional sympathy for a parent who just lost her child. Although, he was facing extreme scrutiny for his actions and acquittal, there was still the fact that this woman lost her only son and will not be able to find any closure. This was a personal thought of mine. There were so many questions I wanted to ask but didn't wish to get into because I knew there would never be an answer to anything I inquire about. Just as the millions of questions Mike Browns family and others had wondered about that went ignored. Questions about that day, the events that took place, and what really happened.

The thing that had struck me and the people of America the most wasn't the fact that this officer wasn't indicted. It was the fact that no case was presented in opposition to the defense. The prosecutor, for the first time I could honestly recall, didn't present any case against the officer at all. He didn't present any argumentation, any witnesses, or cement charges that would have at least granted a case to be sought out. What happened to the practice that's usually an exertion in the court room when it comes to anyone else? What happed to the justice that's usually seek with no abandonment when there's a Black person who's the defendant? It's hard to believe that a prosecutor would try a case at the grand jury without any probable cause to proceed with the hearing. It's unknown. We all watch cop shows where the criminal or individual has to be let off the hook because the prosecutor doesn't have a case. Some of us has even been in a situation where our lives were being determined by the court system. If the prosecutor doesn't have any solid evidence the case never would have made it to the grand jury, especially if there were nothing at all to go off of. So how did it make it to that point without anything to refute or produce? Did the prosecutor even know what side he was arguing for? Did he understand who he was representing, or did he forget that Gary Wilson was the defendant and not Mike Brown? Did he convict so many Black people that he didn't think he'd have to represent one? It's apparent that he didn't do his job. There were other prosecutors that appeared on news stations and other broad castings who also acknowledged his failure to up hold his responsibilities as an attorney of the court. There were no cross examinations, or anyone brought to testify in Mike Browns defense. What happened to all the people who gave their account of what had taken place? What happened to all the people who were threatened by the Ferguson police department for wanting to come forth with the truth? How could there not be one person willing to testify when it's easy for the prosecutor to get ten people to testify against a Black man who they never witnessed do anything? I just kept thinking to myself, "was it really that hard to get a hold of those people that was willing to share their stories with the news reporters who couldn't do anything about the situations (other than bring awareness to what was happening in Ferguson), rather than talk to someone who could do more. Were these "witnesses" who saw the incident only willing to provide insight or did they wish for the young man to receive the justice he deserved and would have wanted for their child if they had suffered the same fate? Were they summoned to come forth, did they refuse, what happened to them? Tell us something because we wish to know the truth just as Mike Brown's family. None of what transpired made any sense.

I wanted to acknowledge the protestors that took to the streets seeking answers. I wanted to remind the readers of peaceful practice that kept the world aware of the crisis at hand. The young people who participated in the demonstration with picket signs and slogans on their t-shirts to demand justice and change the way they were being targeted by police officers. Those who weren't convinced about the decision that freed Gary Wilson. Those who weren't convinced that their lives were safe. I wanted to accredit the Black lives movement because it was truly something I was proud to see. Though unfortunately, I couldn't be a part of it, I felt as if I could be of benefit with through my skill. I wanted to share my thoughts on why Black lives should always matter. We are just as much a part of this country as anyone else. We've given our blood sweat and tears to this country. We've given much contribution to shape and found this country to be the American dream. We've been a part of the development and ideals which has made this country so amazing. So why is it a question if our lives mater? Why should we feel this way after all we invested into this country? After all we fought for to put the past behind us.

I wanted to insert the positive things that made headlines by protestors. The things that made an impact on the world to take action. Some of the slogan's that were chanted which brought the world closer and the realization that wasn't being addressed or resolved. Other countries even begin to acknowledge what was happening in America to the Black youth or Black people as a whole. How could peace be expected if there's no justice being afforded. How could there not be equal rights given to those in grief in any offense whether it's a crime committed by a Black or White person? Or anyone for that matter?

I wanted to address the issue concerning the business owner's and automobiles that were burned or destroyed in the chaos. As well as the opprobrious looters and vandalism who used this tragedy for an opportunity to cause damage or theft. This was a time for unification and change. It was a time to abolish cruel practices and uplifting a people who are tired of the conditions their living in. It was a time for growth and empowerment. And the mourning of a child's life. Not to act uncivilized. Destroying things won't bring any good to a situation, nor will it bring back the life that was lost. The people who property was destroyed wasn't responsible for Mike Brown's death.

They weren't responsible for the acquittal of the officer. Some of the businesses and automobiles were owned by Black people which showed the ignorance of those who didn't care for the injustice that was shown to other Blacks. They didn't care who they caused damage to. They were only concern with their self-gain. This conduct was a contradiction to everything those protestors stood out there fighting for. It showed a lack of discipline and understanding. And most of all it showed a lack of cultural uniform. No one should be the target of senseless crimes or discrimination. How should we expect to be viewed as a people when we can't act like human beings? How should we expect people to treat us fairly when our behavior isn't proper? There's no way any one should have been displaying such selfish characteristic's when the lives of our youth are being considered. Of course, we can't expect to act civilized when we are not treated in such a manner. But we must be better leader's then to confirm the stereotypes held against us. Pain could incite people to do the most unreasonable things. Especially when that pain has been accumulating for some time. It's not to make excuses for what's been done but to acknowledge that when a person mind is conflicted sometimes they can target the wrong source for their anger. I don't condone the actions of those who behaved criminally in no way. I realized that our ill intent could never be productive or a stable desire. It will only cause suffering to the person and those close to them. But in this matter, I didn't want to lose focus of the true antagonism of the chain of events. I wanted readers to know that the cost hurts everyone when vengeance is sort to gain. Vengeance is a blind emotion of anger. It's uncontrollable and at times unmanageable. It's a liability to everyone including the person themselves.

In this poem, I wanted to point out that regardless of our commitment to change the views and actions of people that we are still losing young Black lives or Black lives period. There is more needed to be done. There are other measures that needs to be considered. It seems as if these protestations aren't helping to stop the murders that keeps occurring. I wanted to say that maybe Ferguson needed to be burnt to the ground though I know it's wrong. I wanted to say that maybe some drastic actions needed to be taken in order for our results to be different. But savagery shouldn't ever be mimicked or resorted to. The only way to receive better we must show that we deserve better. Apologies to those who businesses and vehicles were ruined by the Ferguson incident. And rest in peace to Mike Brown and may his family find the strength they need.

Painted by America

Paint me with a bleach perception,

A Caucasian perspective in which I am a threat and should be treated oppressive,

Paint me with a deep misconception; a white man's truth that's mostly deceptive,

See through the eyes of those who possess a brush that is disguised to color the lies,

And cover the cries echoing throughout the ghettos; falling rebels who demise continue to be in vain,

Slain by the intangible weapon's that's more dangerous than those that take aim,

Painted with the blood that stains,
The blood of those imposed upon and stripped of the liberty to be,

The brutal heinous blood shed it took for us to be free,
The sacrifices of early generations,

The unbalanced scale that seems to have a higher persecution of minorities then fair penalization,

The secrets that continue to be whispered,

The painted walls in late November that will always be remembered,

Paint me with a swarthy image,
A sullen description that is horridly wicked,

Paint me with the shades that are appalling to witness,

While you hide behind the paint brush with the skeletons you made victims,

Coated with a sickness,
Devoted to a pigment,

That's chosen to be offensive,
Rose from thee incentive,

And though we're far from slave conditions the hate remains relentless,

Paint me till the makeup of fabricated mixtures you applied are finished,

Till I'm just a work of art that never gets attention,

Though I exist even if the acknowledgement isn't given,

So, paint me with your cruelest affliction,

But forever I'll remain the coolest addition to your painted system.

P.O.A.P

Painted by America

THE BREAK DOWN

In this poem I wanted to try to produce the image of a painting. I wanted to show a portrait of how black people are perceived here in America. The stereotypes that we receive. The misconceptions that we are defined by. And the false justification that describe our circumstances. I wanted to convey the misconstruction that most people judge us with. The views that are bias and the critique which is condemning. I wanted this painting to display the antagonizing dislikes we are colored with that causes hatred towards us. The views that makes us subjected to oppression, discrimination, and malice. I wanted to articulate the image that captures the best artful expression with diction. And convey an ideal of a painter depicting his wrong that speaks out against the cruel behavior inflicted by the paint brush he's using. A paint brush which is meant to describe his actions. This is a painter who is presenting the most negative concept through his botched drawing. An outline of his malicious actions that have offended others. I wanted to capture the story behind that painting and translate that artful expression which is speaking out against the cruel brush the painter is using. The brush that is used to cover his shame and paint over the cruelty he has displayed. This is an abstract painting that has too many conceptual mixtures consisting of the opinions others deem to be approving or unworthy. Opinions that are judgmental and is decorated to a standard of acceptance they believe would make us suitable or appropriate in what is considered to make their "ideal country perfect". A painting that is brilliantly expressed though the picture isn't close to being a master piece. It's cruelly illustrated and repulsively appalling to watch. It incites the anger and aggressive nature which causes others to approach with caution. Or treat us like a high-risk threat and gun us down because of what we're perceived as. It's a painting consisting of scanty beliefs used to produce a visual that projects the discouragement of other's self-esteem. It's about the way we're painted with the different labels in America. And the misrepresentation we're depicted by.

Painted by America is a metaphor used to express the way we are treated, regarded, and premised. It's a phrase that describes the canvas of life, and the human painter who has influenced its figuration with the unpleasant colors of their actions or offensively vivifying expressions. It's a figure of speech pertaining to the way we're being portrayed through an unjust portrait. A portrait that shows a display of discernment, and the affliction being endured, which is painted by the aggrieved, who is responsible for the perception we're viewed by.

The introduction of this poem is a broad statement made to address the issues of what is assumed to be the perception of America. Society has embedded an ideal of what Americans should look like, sound like, and act like. As if the proprieties which are acceptable is only associated with a particular group that represents America. We are persuaded through commercialism and other forms of propaganda that having pale skin, blond hair, blue eyes, or a slim fit is the true illustration of what being an American consist of. We are led to believe that if we don't have any of those traits we don't truly qualify as an American or could have an equally fair life here. We are painted with a bleach perception to believe that we must change certain things about ourselves in order to identify with, or be accepted by, white society. Consumerism wants us to believe that the lighter in complexion we are the more successful or beautiful we'll be. But success comes with trial and isn't procured through favoritism. And beauty has no distinct color or appearance and is the most indecisive quality.

Society is given the impression that black people are a threat. That we are animals and should be put down and treated like menace or a danger to the community. That we're dangerously violent and should be approached aggressively with the intent to harm or injure. We are treated like monsters who haven't been provided any mercy. We are assumed guilty as suspects before being presumed innocent as civilians with rights. We are considered an endangerment to the welfare of others because of the way we dress or look. We are approached aggressively with caution and perceived as a high risk rather than a victim or bystander. We're viewed as if we are ruthless or uncompassionate human beings who have no control of our emotions or actions. We're figured to have malicious intentions to cause hurt or damage to other individuals even though our motives are positive. But why all these false perceptions of us? How is it that we've come to be defined by these misconceptions when we're being treated far viciously then any labels we could be equated to? For years black people have been portrayed as the most atrocious group of people, even upon arriving to America. We have been compared to animals in every sense. And treated even worse. We've been described with every liken tending to cause belittlement, humiliation, or suffering. But why? Is it to convince society that we deserve such discriminatory practice or heinous assaults? Is it to encourage the hatred that's directed towards us? We are continuously oppressed with an injustice that burdens our communities because we are viewed through these misperceptions that are a misrepresentation of who we are. This misinterpretation that is deeply rooted and has become an attachment due to the years of stereotyping. The lies that are hidden beneath their so-called truths exposing the hatred that encourages the malicious labelling which makes us targets of misconception.

If you could look through the eyes of a painter and see the true inspiration of his vision. The motivation that makes him determined, or the encouragement that gives him that drive, do you think that it would be disguised behind a false belief that compels his creativeness? Or would his passion be evident? When looking through the eyes of those with criminal motives, you could see what they disclose. Though their expressions are meant to cover the truth, their eyes reveal it all. It's no different from a painter who is an imposter. He wishes to project the most exquisite portrait though his deception by filling in the details of the picture to disguise the mistakes beneath what may appear to be drawn as perfection. The intentional errors are cloaked with each stroke of the brutal paint brush to give a less immoral portrayal in order to enshroud the cries of the people who are being misrepresented and mistreated. The people who have died because of these vain perceptions or associations. The people who continue to be slain by the weapon's that are devised in secrecy to target them. The weapon's that are deadlier then firearms when they're mentally used to conspire.

The color used in this painting isn't from one of the hues of different pigment mixtures used to make up tinctures in a spectrum, it's from the massacres that has been spilled throughout times. It's the red coagulated color that has been shed from the bodies that have sacrificed their lives or has been spilled in our struggles. It's the blood of those that were taken advantage of and stripped of their liberty to be. The liberty to live as free citizens without being harassed, segregated by racism, or slain unjustly. The heinous blood shed that we are painted with, which reminds us of a horrific past. The blood of those who are unfairly persecuted rather than given an equitable penalization. It's the blood that has made this portrait more realistically then the norm and easy to identify the pain.

The secrets that continue to be whispered are the conspiracies that are assumed. The schemes that are premeditated to hinder our efforts. The plots that are thought to cause our ruin or demise. It's the unlawful acts that are conspired by a secret society of law makers, employers, and services that has discriminated or treated us cruelly. It's the secrets that are voiced in private to maintain a whispers mutter.

The "painted walls in November" is referring to the Indians that were slaughtered because of their refusal to give up their land. We all know that November 24th is the national day the thanksgiving ceremonial is held. In 1621, the Indians and pilgrims joined together to give thanks for good harvest and peace. But friendly relations didn't last long because some Europeans cheated the Indians out of their property and took their land. Warfare soon became common as the Indians fought back to preserve what was theirs to claim. Thousands of them were killed in battle from guns and diseases brought to America by the European settlers. The painted walls are the blood shed of the Indians who was also stained by America.

Because we are black we are painted with the darkest image. An image that is described to represent us because of our appearance. An image of gloominess or hopelessness. An image that mirrors stagnation or idleness. An image that is equated with defeat or failure. An image that reflects the complexion of our form that is meant to keep our spirits down and us believing that we are worthless. We are painted with unmerited character that is repulsively repugnant. Character that brings about disgust and disgrace so, that the shades we are covered with are too appalling to witness.

We are being painted with all these perceptions of injustice while the painter hides behind the wicked paint brush that expresses his savagery. The actions that is responsible for the skeletons he now has because, of the victims who were coated due to his sadomasochistic mental sickness. The reason for the blood-letting is because of the painter's desperate urge to dominate and maintain superiority. He's determined to show that he is much better than most others of his kind. He feels that it's his right to conquer or rule over those who do not resemble him or the image he is loyal to. So, the concept he creates in this painting displayed is a perception of his "ideal" reality. A painting that speaks of the tyranny in his quest for control. the oppressive nature is meant to keep others inferior or suppressed from their own independence.

By looking closely in this picture, you would be able to see how we rose up because of the faith that arouse our grit and the belief that drove us to take action against the mischief that is caused to us. Constantly fighting off the torment that is being applied along with the misjudgment that's misconstrued. And though we're far from extreme conditions of servitude it's clearly vivid that the hatred still remains. But regardless if we're painted till the fabricated mixtures of enmity, discernment, or oppressiveness is finish covering us completely, and we're tossed to the side hoping that the truth beneath the layers of this portrait never gets attention. We will always be recognized by the accurate reality of the honest accounts no matter if we're painted with the thickest coating to elude notice of the painful torment we suffer from. And out of every painting that has been artfully depicted by this painter, the individual back ground of this portrait tells the most prevailing story of all the pictures of people that has been wronged by his paint brush.

Floaters

Am I the ridicule of conversation at your so called gatherings?,

Conspiracies of hatred amongst a secret society of hooded racist who's claims are baffling,

Whispers of arrogance heard by travelers of enslavement from visitor's who take ownership of land belonging to early native establishment,

Rather than join the present in harmony; past confabulation poisons the minds of modern white segregationist,

Manipulated by ancient cruel niggerly habits which influence a new generation of disorient savages,

Those who conceal their discernment out of mere embarrassment,

In order to avoid criticism and being scrutinized by the rest of the world who views racism through the eyes of infuriated activist,

So, both sides of adversaries; supremacist and those without equable differences; are compromise by these adaptors who possess a floaters alliance to whomever their gathered with instead of having an equilibrium opinion,

When the topic of hate is mentioned; it's concurred by the proportion whose bigotry steams from not wanting to be viewed as an antagonist,

Caught in between one's aversion of color and another's repugnance for the ignorance projected by other's,

In hopes to be accepted due to their bias portrayal and their moral betrayal which makes them bi-racial occasionally when they're not pretending to be an advocate,

Or anyway you have it,
Yet the disrespect can't be neglected; and mentally I'm not relieved of the discriminatory practice,

So, I'm led to believe there's more truth then you wish for me to perceive in your actions,

Cause even acting can be real; that's why stunt doubles are often cast for a roll just in case of an accident,

So, I won't give you the satisfaction of letting you off the hook,

In this catch and release stream; racism will no longer be overlooked,

Despite your innocent claims of your conduct being misunderstood,

Cause what's understood is that you sometimes wear your hood when it's beneficial to your own good,

Tending to alienate or insult me without a care,

Then turn around and befriend me when you assume that the coast is clear,

No longer will I tolerate this bogus snare,

While you play me for the fool and string me by a noose when you're with your own peers,

So, by the honest truth I swear; that every threat will be treated the same even those who presume to be sincere,

So be yourselves even when you don't mean well,

I mean well; conduct yourself how you would act amongst your own equal as if you were around a different race of people,

And maybe then you wouldn't seem so deceitful; or cause me to think your incapable of a genuine friendship that's actually believable.

P.O.A.P

Floaters

THE BREAK DOWN

The ideal of floaters is a concept that speaks about poseurs. It's a poem that addresses the fraudulent associations and insincere bond of friendship that's formed by most white people. People who pretend to be opposed to the racism and discrimination committed against blacks, only when they're not in the presence or company of other bigots. It's about the false impression of comradeship and the affectation that's displayed the unctuous proclaims of desegregation and unity. As well as the unauthentic comportment shown which is thought to be honest. Often black people find themselves on the defense against senseless and unreasonable hatred. We're constantly striving to ward off offensive insults or malicious acts intending to cause us harm. We're continuously confronted by direct attacks of injustice that's obvious to the human eye. It's not usually expected for the threat to exist amongst those we sincerely affiliate ourselves with. It's not thought that we would encounter that kind of discernment or those type of abhorrent characteristics within our circle of friends. A circle that is presumed to be mutually genuine and free of any loathe or bias judgement. But from time to time we experience a pattern of treachery and broken trust. I wanted to talk about the amicable portrayal that's extended and the duplicitous behavior that's questionable. The actions that causes us to reevaluate, reconsider, and relinquish the companionship we built with most white people found to be floaters. Floaters are individuals who wander about aimlessly without a fixed course of loyalty. Moving back and forth to whatever devotion they feel is convenient for them.

It's a person who straddles the fence of morality to avoid excoriation or shame.

I wanted to start this poem off with a thought of there being a secret meeting held with racist individuals gathered together discussing conspiracies of hatred. A meeting consisting of actual hooded bigots and hypocrites who are sometimes racist when they're around the influences of other's who dictate their beliefs or values. It's truly perplexing to imaging these same people who claim to stand for equality and harmony, assembled with segregationist. It's very disappointing and infuriating to know that you've trusted in someone who been dishonest with you. Someone you assumed had shared the same views and understanding only to realize that they've been deceiving you the entire time.

I wanted readers to have two perceptions in mind when they imagine this meeting taking place. I wanted to try to present that picture of a bunch of Klan's men disguised behind hoods to hide their true identity. The identity they conceal is a representation of their false intentions which describes the relationship formed with floaters. And the hood being a reference to their actions which covers the insincere motives beneath the surface. I also wanted to articulate a visual of that meeting taking place in a dining room setting with slave owners gathered together conversing about dynamics of slavery and other things while in the company of slaves who serviced them and attended to their duties. You can imagine the audacity and discourtesy these men demonstrated while in the company of slaves who overheard some of these conversations that took place. Back then in earlier times, slave was thought to be insignificant and weren't respected as people. They didn't have a voice, so it didn't matter whether they were present or not during certain discussions. I wanted to convey a theory of what might have taken place years ago. What we could assume is going on right under our nose now. Them travelers of enslavement being us and those visitor's being the same group of racists joined together at those tables now, still claiming ownership of a land that has never belonged to them. Still plotting ways to keep us enslaved. And still conversing about matters that were meant to keep us inferior to them.

Rather than embrace each other in harmony and accept the perception of today's society. Those same bitter talks of enmity continue to be instilled in most of the mindless people who refuse to grow with the rest of the world. Those past confabulations of hatred and malignancy once expressed are still being passed on to people of our generations poisoning their perception of unity. People who shouldn't see the world through the eyes of past segregationist and old bitter people but instead, view them through modern cohesion that has been an example of equity, prosperity, and progression we could accomplish as a collective whole.

But we are often manipulated by former habits of deception and convinced to believe that we can trust in these individuals known as floaters. These descendants of nefarious savages are more obedient to an ideal which persuade them to carry out the same malevolent treatment their ancestor's displayed.

The only difference from old bigots and these floaters is that they conceal their discernment out of mere embarrassment in order to avoid criticism and being scrutinized by the rest of the world who is presented with the awareness of racism by people who protest and fight actively to make a difference. Unlike past times, racism could be examined by a vast proportion of the world's population because of technology and efforts of global awareness. In today's times, being a racist could hurt a person's brand or business so, people tend to disclose or hide their hatred to keep from being boycotted or picketed against. These floaters sometimes have a strategic motive to use black people for their self-gain. In order to get the support of other black consumers or investor's. But they honestly don't have any interest in being a true friend.

So, both sides, meaning racist and those who believe in equality are compromised by these adaptors because of their indecisiveness. They are not only perceived as floaters because of their disloyalty to minorities but, also because of their inconsistent hatred which can't be balanced. There's no way anyone could say their a racist but entertain the company of a person or a thing they claim to possess aversion for. Rancor is something that could never be suppressed to tolerate that which is considered to be antagonizing or provokes animosity. So, the expressions or actions will show in a person's comportment when hate is something that they feel. Which rules out the notion of floaters being hateful people. Their just loyal to the ideal of being viewed in regard to their own kind. So, when the topic of hate is mentioned to them by other white segregationist, they agree in order to be spared of any hostility or to seem like their traitors to their own kind.

Their caught in between this dispute of morality hoping to be accepted by both parties which makes them "bi-racial" when they're not pretending to express their concerns for the unfair treatment or acknowledgement of minorities.

Anyway, it's perceived or examined, the disrespect of allowing this kind of behavior or any other, to continue to be eluded or ignored is completely nocuous. It gives the impression that the exception of racism is extended to those who pretend to be affiliates or poses as brethren of ours. Regardless of what we chose to neglect or exclude their intent will still remain the same. And mentally we could never be relieved of the discriminatory practice that's done behind our backs. Because we have no choice but to believe that there's more truth to their actions then they wish for us to perceive even if they're not entirely hateful people. Because whether their literally actor's or metaphorically speaking it's no difference since people also get hurt in the process of performing

I wanted to make it clear that I don't believe that any racism should be let off the hook. So much so, that the reference of a catch and release stream is made to indicate that even though it may be accepted by most, I would never overlook the fact that the act was still committed. I think that it's extremely stupid and very simple minded of a person to allow themselves to be driven by something so foolish as a color to harbor abhorrent for another race of human beings. I believe that it should be illegal even if it was just a thought to carry out the intent. Just because the action isn't on purpose doesn't mean that it wasn't deliberate despite any innocent claims of their conduct being mistaken as intentional. What's understood is that an act is only committed because of intention.

And it's clear that these floaters sometimes wear their hoods when it suits them.

When these floaters are in the presence of other racist individuals, they develop the same characteristic's. They act as if they never considered you a friend. They make a hostile situation out of what was once peaceful just to show that their companionship was just an act. But got the nerve to pretend that their behavior was meaningless when the cost is clear. But no longer should this false trap be permitted. No longer should we allow this type of individuals to play us for an idiot while our people continue to be stringed up by a noose when they're with a group of bigots who actually wish to execute expressions of hatred.

So, I swear by the truth, that every threat will be treated just the same whether it's intentional or not. Whether it's planned or presumed to be a misunderstanding. So be yourselves even when you don't mean to come off as a racist or a person of ignorant belief. I mean, conduct yourself how you would act amongst your own race of people just as you would around us in order for us to perceive you as the true person you present yourself to be. And maybe then you wouldn't seem so mendacious or snaky. And cause me to assume that your incapable of a sincere friendship that's actually believable.

The Jezebel Pt.3

So, what if you don't meet my perception of what negate a Jezebel due to your unusual indiscretions,

Being that you fit what's been projected you feel as though; who am I to make you feel like you need an introspection,

But it's because of your disregards for fidelity and union; along with your indulgence in a vulgar perspective that's mainly rejected,

Not to mention your oversexed unacceptance which is why other women are disrespected,

Defiling yourself for the pleasures of instant gratification,

Or compensation that could never remunerate in payment,

As if your body has a price that could be purchased through solicitation,

Selling your chastity for a fee that buys your degradation,

But it's your proclamation so you live according to your statement,

By sleeping with other women mates; with no regards if they were taken,

Hoping to supplant their position by not having any modest limitations,

But a Jezebel is a woman who desires endless copulation,

Never easily satiated,
She's truly a freak for disgrace,

Extremely explicit with her actions and even lewder than they say,

Cause for a jezebel it takes practice and she's improving each day,

She's a temptress that could easily sway true love to go astray,

She's the one who is indecent and has her body on display,

She's the one who can't be saved; because she feels free to be depraved,

She behaves in treacherous ways,
She's the foul labels they equate,

The names that bring women shame; but she isn't blamed or defamed because we think all women relate,

So, she escapes without a trace; cause we can't recognize her traits,

And she dissimulates in the stereotypes while we continue this debate,

Cause she refuse to show her face; so, every woman bares disgrace,

But she's the one that we embrace; while other women are debased,

She's the jezebel!
But we don't know her too well; cause we give women hell,

We judge them all no different from each other being we couldn't tell,

But if we read this well and pay attention to what's been mentioned; we'll be able to know the difference between our women and the one called The Jezebel.

The Jezebel

THE BREAK DOWN

In this poem I wanted to speak about the women who should be judged as "The Jezebel". The women that we misconstrued with those who aren't scandalous. I gave my thoughts and opinions on what should separate the label of a Jezebel from modest women who hasn't offended or personally wronged anyone during their sexual prowls. The women who have a triumphant past and continue to shine bright in our preceding future. The women who just wish to suffice their desire to be loved or intoxicated with lust. Now I wanted to show "The Jezebel" we should scrutinize for her conduct. The women who behaves disgracefully. I wanted to describe the nature of "The Jezebel" and how her actions differ. I wanted to remove the cloak I believe she hides behind. The cloak which represents the shadow of decent women who are represented by the Jezebel's comportment. I wanted to make a distinction that would set women apart from the humiliating and insulting names they are branded with. It's in the Jezebel's nature to display an excessive urgency to satisfy her craving. Cravings that are pursued shamefully. They have an urge to be impress or impelled to some course or activity. It's those unapologetic or careless characteristic's that shows their distinguished mark, the desire that drives or urge them forward or on. No pun intended.

The moderate indulgence other women may engage in from time to time in a more tasteful manner, shouldn't be viewed with extreme aversion. We hold women to a standard of expectation that is always re-adjusted to guarantee their failure. We expect their perfection when the world isn't perfect. Whether their decorum is publicly shown modestly and respectfully, we still find a way to denounce them. These modest indulgences are not sexual extremes. There not dishonorable or tasteless representations unlike the actual Jezebel. There the actions of average women who limit themselves to the effect pleasure would have on them. Or the scope people would view them by. Only to still be judged as a Jezebel.

I wanted to unclothe the Jezebel for who she is, so that these moderate women could stop being shamed for the actions of those who have no dignity or moral decency. Those who are more repulsive and disorderly. In the first poem I showed the women who are considered to be moderate in their sexual pursuits. The women who achieved great establishment and recognition which was mentioned in the second poem. The women we disparaged because of our failure to see them with the respect they deserve. The acknowledgement they should receive as a parallel resemblance. Because of "The Jezebel" we are unable to identify those women due to our heedlessness to be men and show the worthy women that they have our support, encouragement, and honor. This poem shows who I feel meets the qualifications of "The Jezebel".

I wanted to make the introduction of this poem personal. I wanted to start off with a clear indication of who I'm referring to. And let the true Jezebel know that I'm aware of her and the lewd comportment she demonstrates. The names that she refuses to own up to. The stereotypes she has become complacent with being that other women bare most of her shame. I wanted her to know that she could no longer hide in the shadows of decent women. I'm revealing her for the sleazy and demoralized disobedient she is.

By acknowledging my thoughts of those who are judged as a Jezebel has caused her actions to stand out. And now she is forced to take a look at herself. She sees that her actions are far too opprobrious. But she feels like who am I to make her feel like she needs an introspection? Who am I to judge her? Who am I to cause the world to stop and take notice. But I don't intend to judge her, I just want to set her apart from the faultless women who continue to suffer because of the misconceptions she's responsible for. Her disregards for devotion or commitment. Her involvement in the obscenities that is condemned by society. Not to mention her sexual insatiability that's rash which cause most people to view women alike. I wanted to change that perception and stop her behavior from affecting other's. She's the one defiling herself just to receive some form of pleasure whether it's money, spitefulness, or satisfaction. While other women are being blamed. While their baring her guilt. But she doesn't care. She doesn't see anything wrong with selling herself as long as she benefits in some way. But she could never be or feel reimburse for her debauchery. As if her chastity should be solicited to the highest bidder for the price of being humiliated and belittled.

It's kind of a public statement she's officially making by living her life the way she desires. Even if that means sleeping with other women companions regardless if there married or not. A Jezebel sometimes have spiteful intentions to cause a relationship to divide. Sometimes she feels that she can be the better woman. She feels she can give a man what other women aren't willing to give. And that's all of herself without any restraints. But a Jezebel needs are too demanding for any single particular male to conform to. She is willing to disgrace herself in order to fulfill her own desires. And is willing to go the length of the most debasing character just to show how compelling her urge is. It can't be controlled or tamed. And when the attempt to contain it is made, it only increases in its sultry provocation. And what people usually equate to women of more dignified moderation is actually a polite description if intending to define the Jezebel. She's truly more iniquitous then one can assume. She's more characterless then they can compare. She's been practicing all her life due to each experience she's been through. And she's been through so much that she feels indecent herself. So, she acts the part. But she can't stand the sight of who she truly is. So, she tries to blend in with other women who are not piously defloured but, indulge in sexual behavior that's may be frown upon. She's the temptress so she's very persuasive. She can convince any man through flirtation and sexual favors to shift their affection or breach their vows. She's the one who leaves little to the imagination. Incredibly sexy, has true potential to be better than how she perceives herself, but is psychologically damaged to the point that she can't see her life without such repulsive behavior. It's the only way she knows how to feel free. She doesn't know anything else since she was forced to adapt to her circumstances. So, she doesn't see a need to suddenly change. She behaves in ways that most people don't approve of. Letting men violate her in the most demeaning way. Sharing her among the crew. Cheating on their partners with others because settle down just isn't them. She's the one they actually mean to condemn. But she hides in the shadows of every woman who isn't a virgin, married or commit adultery, nor are adhering to the conformity of decorum. She's the one deserving of the foul labels they use to stereotype women who don't display her characteristic's. She represents those names that brings those women shame. The shame that they are innocent of. But she isn't the one censured because we think all women relate. So, we mistakenly judge wrongly which causes her to go unnoticed because we can't determine the distinctions that separate women conduct. So, the Jezebel takes the appearance of respectable women who intentions are always honest in their sexual pursuits. Since the Jezebel refuse to show her face these women somehow earns her disgrace. She doesn't wish to be singled out. She's always been selfish when it comes to getting what she wants. So, every woman that is associated to her nature shares this humiliating disgust.

This is the identity of the true Jezebel in case you haven't notice. And even if we feel we do we could never assume we know her well enough being that we give hell to all the women we misjudged. We think of them all to a degree of being a Jezebel by the way we treat them. Women have been demeaned and vilified for so long that it's become a norm for society to devalue them. But if we read this well enough to get a better understanding of what qualifies a Jezebel then we'll be able to know how to detect those who are worthier of our respect then we grant them.

The conversation pt3: past and present

You have a collect call from: "youngster". An inmate at a federal institution. To accept please dial five now.

(youth) Hello?

(elder) Hey there youngster, how you hanging in there?

(youth) I could complain about a million reasons of why I don't want to be here,

But it's too late to realize my stubborn immaturity and the fact I didn't see clear,

Instead of taking heed I chose to belie; instead of being patient I chose the street; instead of doing right it seems like I chose everything that was wrong for me.

And now prison time is a constant reminder of the greatest mistake in my life that hunts me every time I close my eyes when I lay down to sleep,

Would you believe I'm told when to move – when to go – when to eat?,

What to wear – how to act – and how to speak?,

This isn't what I imagined would happen just to make sure that my family is replete,

(elder) Everyone makes mistakes including me; I was no different; I didn't listen neither to the advice that was given to me,

That's why I made it my business to instruct you positively; so that the cycle doesn't repeat,

So that you don't become me years later after your free,

So that you realize your stupidity would be the one sad quality that cause you grief; so that you wouldn't have to look at your past; just to tell him though your future maybe bright your naïve actions will cost you bad,

And though you had good intentions; nothing pertaining to the street ever last,

And that it isn't worth the time spent out of mind; confined to a cell hoping that the days doesn't drag,

Because the desire to be free is something you desperately wish you had,

But I'll never put you down because of an error; But now it's up to you to teach the right way to the next era,

(youth) How am I suppose to do that when I haven't even begun to make my own life better?,

(elder) Trust me you'll think of something clever; I know because me and you are not too different from one another,

In fact, you're the same young brother I used to be; and now you are me after changing what we used to be,

These conversations between past and present was just to acknowledge how much we grew to be,

And the message I would convey to a youthful me if I could go back and amend the mistakes I made foolishly.

P.O.A.P

The Conversation: Past and present

THE BREAK DOWN

In this conversation, I wanted to show the reader's that these confabulations weren't only about the fight to save our youth. It has also been about a man identifying with his past and address the mistakes he made as a young teen. Most times during a minute of reflection after making an error, we dwell on the activities that were done. The blunders that cost us dearly. And the choices we've made that were faulty. We imaging the wrong we've did and often wish we can go back and correct them. Well in this case, it was one of those wishes a person sometimes would hope for. A chance to go back and have a conversation with their youthful selves. They imagine the chance of going back to rectify some of the reckless behavior due to ignorant decisions. It's a known fact that in reality the past can't be changed nor amended. But I wanted to give an ideal of how that conversation would have went. How the reenactment of the most unfortunate decision would have been. In this poem I wanted to sum up all three of these conversations by showing that we all make choices as a youth out of heedlessness and stubbornness due to what we believe at the time. And nothing would be able to change our path but, experience and maturity. I also want to show that process or turning point where we realize our error's but, don't get to express the feeling of how much we screwed up. We could never find it in ourselves to forgive our self for the damage inflicted. I wanted to give the reader's a thought of self-realization. Where the conscious becomes a clear thought and we see our errors for what their worth.

I wanted to show the consequence of our error's as a result to the wrong choices we make. I wanted it to be clear for all reader's that every action has an effect just as every decision has an outcome. I wanted it to be noted that this conversation wasn't happening on a comfortable plate form or a suitable environment. I wanted to show that despite the difference between the young man and the elder, that there has always remained a level of respect and acknowledgement that they honored. They've always shared an inseparable bond that kept their communication strong. And this made the relationship between these two individuals more understanding of how familiar they were.

I wanted to show how the young man's life turned out as a result of his decisions that stagnated his past. I wanted to show how he devoted himself to change so that he could probably one day help some other young man just like him. I wanted to show the regret that is harbor due to an extremely foolish mistake. And the suffering that's usually endure because of uneducated decisions and our failure to listen to what's right. I wanted to show this young man's acknowledgement for what he's done and how his patience should have been more poise. How the newly conditions affected him. Not just his sleep but, his lack of conscious awareness of his choices. The young man expresses his shock for the way things function when you're in an uncomfortable setting that suppresses your limitations. An institutional setting that bounds your movement. He couldn't imagine this would be the severity of the consequence even though he knew there was some form of punishment. Sometimes we may not know the length or effect our actions will cost us. But it doesn't mean that we should, in order to know that it's wrong. Unfortunately, it takes the most depriving situation to wake us up. But we cannot begin to change the way we think or act until we accept some accountability for the choices we make. We often live with regrets even if we've made the necessary adjustments conducive to our productiveness. Because our character defines the person we are.

I wanted to find a point to reveal the true identity of the young man who has always been the elder. I wanted to write something meaningful but show that this was just a reflection of the elders' past and how he conducted himself today versus the behavior he displayed as a younger man. It was a reason why he made it his "Personal business" to instruct the young man. It's a reason he didn't want for the cycle to repeat. Not just because he wanted to save other young man but, because he didn't wish to commit the same error's that would lead him back to prison. He wanted to show his younger self that he has changed the mentality he once had and isn't making those mistakes anymore. That he hadn't listened once but now he takes heed to every advice that's given.

He lets his younger self know how great he's turned out. And that he was always clever, he just didn't apply himself to the right cause. He advises himself that he can change the misdirection's of some of the young men in the world or that are in his situation. When the youth begin to realize his reason for being there, it was the elder looking to be reminded of his purpose. His desire to make a difference for other's.

The young man realized that nothing could truly last when it pertains to the streets as the elder once said. And now after becoming an adult he realizes that every good intention could have a great risk when the pursuit is negative. And it was now up to him to show the right way to the new era which is the next generation of young men.

I wanted to show when the young man first acknowledge his need to change. When he stated that he hadn't begun to work on himself, it indicated that there was some improvement needed to be made in order to better his life. And the elder's acknowledgement of the fact his younger self would turn out great, only confirm how it would turn out for him.

I wanted to give reader's an account of an actual situation while showing a person reflecting on a moment of their past and having the urge to change certain things about their former behavior. This is The Conversation Past and Present.

Judge Me Not

Look into my eyes and you'll see pain,
You'll see bloodshed and anger,

You'll see a lot of things that define me but you're just a critic looking to find blame in someone other than yourself,

Rather point the finger of reproof being that is suits you,

Mainly because culpability isn't something that your use to,

And now that you can pass judgement instead; it seems to be something that amuse you,

Well then; is a hypocrite any better than the one who makes an error?,

Or is the one with fault inculpable enough to determine the case of another?,

Because if the guilty is left to condemn the accused; how then could there ever be a fair hearing when misery expects company to share its gloom?,

No saints in the room just a bunch of politics,

All gathered in a breath of blogger's and twits,

The age of internet glitz,
The pre-judged who only wish to be judged,

And rule out those who just happen to be judged,

Now that's three judged if you ask the question; but honestly, I'm not here to be judge,

Because that would make me exactly like the contradiction this poem speak of,

The lynch mob that's corrupt,
The founding fathers of miscreants whose iniquity we can't seem to trust,

So, stop the stoning and drop the mineral's,
If it's knowledge we seek then let it be told from wiser views who aren't themselves criminals,

Individuals with gavels in jail strips who like to badger for clues during the interview,

Magistrate's but not suitable,
Judges who judge me and you in truth when their actions aren't dutiful,

So please would you judge me not.

P.O.A.P

Judge Me Not

THE BREAK DOWN

This poem touches on the general matter of being judged by people who are just as erring and blameworthy but, people who tend to think their better then other's as if they're infallible or innocent. The type of individuals who point their fingers to divert the focus of censure. Or disparage other's as if there a better example of good character. Those who portray an image as if they're holier than thou or pious enough to decide the case of another. This is about the critics who find a reason to place judgement, condemning those in error while their hands hide the guilt they commit. People who chide other's just to feel good about themselves when they're just as guilty or live with faults of their own. I wanted to speak about the hypocrites who disguise themselves as saints when they're not in the seat of scrutiny or being scolded for their blunders. Many times, you find people playing judge and jury in situations when they're no better than the person they're shaming.

If you look into a person's eyes you may see the pain they've suffered, you may see the difficult they've faced, you may even see the bloodshed and anger they've experience along with every other thing they could have possibly went through. You may see a lot of things that define them or made them who they are but, whenever an individual is looking to find a reason to criticize someone, it only means that they already have a negative perception of them. They already see fault in their character before it's detected. They've already judged them before actually getting to know them or finding out if what their accused of is valid. Most times these critic's look to find fault in someone other than themselves.

They view other people in the most disreputable way, not giving them a chance to make their own impression. They rather point their fingers being that their reason to reproof suits them more then affording anyone fair judgement. Mainly because they're not use to culpability. They've been denying their own wrong for so long that they refuse to believe that people would provide an honest perception of who they are. So, they judge in a sense of them lacking truth with in them self. And if it was a case of determining ones faults their amused to be on the critiquing end rather than the accused because it makes them feel better about the wrong they've done.

Honestly, is a hypocrite any better than the one who makes an error? Is the wicked any better than the one who live foul? How then is the one with fault worthy enough to decide if someone else actions are vile. If the guilty is suited to condemn the accused, how could there ever be a fair process of judgement, when those who are corrupt can't be trusted to make a righteous decision? Misery loves company and so does those who are condemned.

There's never any saints present when one is being judged because nobody's perfect. And even those of religious devotion knows that god is the only virtuous judge. It's just a bunch of opinionated people gathered in a breath of bloggers and twits, who think there more pious then those denounce or accused of misconduct. It's almost exactly like what's going on today with the social sites of the internet, and everyone who have something to say about the next person, when they're far from perfect themselves. They've been judged before for things that are displeasing and maybe even disgraceful. They've once been the one who was accused or hid their faults in the dark. There the pre-judged who now wish to be judge. They wish to examine other's instead of being under the scope. Their eager to rule out those who just happen to be judged. But how could that not be looked at as absurd? How could that be looked at as a fair determination.

I'm not here to judge anybody. I'm not here to be the contradiction this poem speaks of. I am no better than the people being judged nor those doing the castigating. I am just advising that people take a look in the mirror before pointing out what's wrong with other's. Before gathering together a lynch mob for persecution. These founders of judgement build their case on false grounds being that their structure lacks guiltlessness. So, their foundation of proof can't be taken as factual. And how could we trust those who view other's as if they can't do any wrong themselves. No one's perfect. So, what entitles them to be judge? I just ask the people to stop the stoning of criticism and drop the mineral's that's intended to hurt other's. Those rocks you keep throwing are the same rocks you should be ducking. Because if it's knowledge we seek to know about the character or conduct of other's. Then let it be told through the findings of those who have a good sense of awareness and are not mentally impure.

These individuals rather possess a gavel from the defendants stand point and play detective although they've been a suspect during or at some time in their life. Their badgering other's as if they were never in the same circumstances. Their impersonating magistrates when they aren't qualified legally or hypothetically. And even if they were, who's to say they're not impeachable? These are dissimulated "judges" who analyze us all in the matter of truth when being honorable can't be obtain if they're not perfect. So, their decision can't be assumed to be absolutely true because their duty to be someone of a pious back ground is scanty. So please, if you're now going to judge me for my thoughts on this just spare me of the hypocrisy.

The Parent Brain

What about the parent brain?
Like; why even acknowledge it?

Shouldn't it be clear he's the responsible one I mean: isn't it obvious?

We know its conscious demeanor and its choices that's positive,

His calculated decision; because he was raised to be this way through maturity and betterment to make a productive living,

Once corrupt himself,
So, he made modifications to build his mind,

That's growth from its delinquent ways?
That's him finding the potential in the volition to change the course of his future mistakes,

That's premonition?
He learned from his childish ways because he decided to listen,

He is the parent brain though,
Thoughtful and kind,

Concerned but wise enough to know not to worry its mind,

But that's being a parent,
That's being aware that the choice you make can't be rewind,

And that's being apparent?
Because the adult brain is the conscious one,

It's accountable for the actions it displays,

That's why its comportment is expressed through safe thinking by being smart in the path it takes,

And I know because all parent brains could relate,

But I don't need the accreditation or commendations followed by what is presented to felicitate,

It isn't about being a parent in the sense of having a child,

It's a matter of being the responsible one who makes sure that the child mind doesn't repeat the same bad decisions that keeps on bringing him down,

I just hate to see the child's mind become another "product" of his so-called environment,

Brought and sold by his erroneous inheritors because of his error's due to its childishness,

But the parent brain ain't one to complain,

It's more for empowerment till the child mind grow up to obtain the same mind frame he maintains,

And that's acknowledgement!
The parent brain.

P.O.A.P

The Parent Brain

THE BREAK DOWN

In this poem I wanted to relate the responsibility of one who is conscience and a conscious thinker. One who makes the right choices that wouldn't result in misfortune, grief, or loss. One who's volition is not followed by error or regrets. One who contemplates the possibilities before choosing to act. And the one who is more aware of the fate of his decisions. It's understood that even when we're thinking productively or in a constructive manner we can still suffer an unfortunate outcome due to the results of our efforts. Sometimes the inevitable can't be avoided. But it's not intentionally, when we use our brain positively, do we incur those calamities on ourselves. I wanted to show the nature of the brain that is mindful of his actions and is considerate of the steps it takes. And more so, a person who cogitates rationally to avoid hindrance or suppressions and putting themselves or other's in a compromising predicament. It's also a comparison between the immaturity of a child and the development of an adult. But it can be anyone who's judgement isn't tainted by capricious urges. It pertains to the inconsideration of one who lacks an obligation to be reliable and the accountability of one who regards all in the choices he makes. It's about one who cares for the growth and development of others. And could be depended on to be sound in judgement and the directions they pursue. This is the parent brain.

At first, I pondered on the thought of how I could convey the perception of such a poem. And what was there to know that isn't already known. Like what about the parent brain. What about the choices someone makes that is always intended to establish structure, order, and produce a better means to live without risking or jeopardizing themselves or those they love. What about their stable way of thinking that prevents devastation or disaster. Honestly, like what is there to know that isn't a constant example of logical reasoning and sound decision making. We see it everyday and every time our actions affect us in impeding ways that let's us know we're not being responsible. We notice it when others constantly tell us what we're doing is a bad idea or wouldn't be a bright alternative. Why acknowledge these wholesome characteristic's that are conducive to our mental effectiveness? Why take notice in the correctness to achieve a desire or to follow a righteous pursuit in the path to procure what we crave. Why take interest in the qualities that would always grant the satisfaction we hope for, and not the disappointment we often do not consider. Why, because it's something we need to know in order to identify those who possess strategic and calculated thinking. It's something we need to know to determine if those in our life are stagnant to our growth or a benefit. We need to know who we can rely on and who we can't. I thought about a few reasons that distinguish the parent brain from the child mind and why it should be obvious, but I wanted to make it apparent for those who fail to realize their distinction.

Shouldn't it be clear that being reliable would qualify one as being susceptible and responsible? I mean we are talking about the parent brain. The parent in the sense of having a duty to show proper conduct through critical thinking. Being careful and precise. Not indulging in frivolous reasoning or becoming a liability to their own or other people furtherance. His conscious demeanor is something that shows his growth. It's something that shows his maturity through his/her thoughts and actions. It shows his awareness of a situation and how to avert or rectify any misunderstanding. It shows his effectiveness in the way he handles a problem, the way he addresses an issue, the way he rationalizes with complicated elements that could impede his/her existence. The choices that are selected which are always positive.

The parent brain is always a calculated individual. Always

contemplating different solutions and possibilities that would bring about affirmative results. He's the one who considers the harm along with the advances and base his decision's off of that which causes the greater damage and not the greater enjoyment. Meaning that even if the benefit out weighed the bad, the slightest danger was still greater than the amount which was gained. And he would choose which caused less expropriation and not what would grant more pleasure because he knows that the cost is more painful even if the gratification seems prodigious. And this is because he was brought up to be more heedful of the things that could cost him severely due to his shortcomings and the blunders he made that influenced him to seek change. But his upbringing isn't referring the way he was raised in this sentence, it's hinting at the way he made the transformation from thinking ignorantly to being more positive. And that's because the parent brain hadn't always been the conscious thinker we come to know. It was once corrupt too. Meaning it was once characterized by improper conduct. It once made those unintelligent choices that deprived him from life advances. It once made immature decision that hindered his ability or prohibited his growth. This parent brain which is metaphor of a human being that has evolved, is someone who wasn't always considerate of their actions or the affect they caused. It's a person who has seen enough of his errors destroy opportunities or relationships that he felt the need to change in order to keep from losing it all or ending up in the same useless situations.

So, the modifications he made to build his mind is so that he could make smarter decisions and think more wisely before acting on his thoughts so that he didn't continue to end up in the same predicament. It's the elevation period of maturity and becoming an adult. Growing up to be thoughtful and dependable. Gaining a circumspection to observe every possible event. And adhering to an obligation to make more brighter judgements. These mental adjustments keep him aware that his choices have ramifications that could ruin great chances. Helping him grow up from them past delinquent ways that once kept him unproductive.

When we begin to take account of our own faults and see the potential in ourselves to change the course of our path by making the right decisions, that's when we begin to evolve. That's when we begin to develop intellectually and determine the accurate volition that prevents idle mistakes. And it's because of the premonition of redundant stumble that we realize that our lives need urgent correction. But that's only if we listen to warnings of those errors and learn from the childish conduct displayed, only then we can begin to make a difference in those patterns.

But the parent brain isn't only conscious of himself. He's almost like an actual parent. He's thoughtful and kind. He's caring and desire nourishment for all because he knows how much a mistake can cost someone or how crucial a decision could be in deciding your fate. He shares the same worries and concerns for everyone else as he does for himself. But he's wise enough to know that not everyone could be saved. Not everyone has understanding or reasoning. Not everyone is willing to heed to sound advice. And he wouldn't allow himself to be driven insane by one's lack of attentiveness. But that's being a parent. All parents worry about their children in the same sense but realize when it's impossible to reach them after every option is exhausted, after every possibility has been seek, they begin to understand that they have to allow them to learn the hard way which is never easy to accept. I read in a book by Sheikh Abdul Azeez ibn Abdullah Ibn Baz about the illness of the mind. And he said: the one with an illness when he understands the illness as well as understanding the cure, is best capable of beginning to utilize the cure and free himself from the illness and it is natural for the intelligent person who prefers life and freedom from illness to give importance to recognizing the illness and knowing it's cure. However, some people have been overtaken by the desire and overwhelmed by it until they become satisfied with it, and, pleased with it, until their perception and awareness had died, thus they do not pay attention to the one who express to them the remedy, as the illness has become normal and natural to them. They are comfortable and content to remain in a corrupt state of mind, having weak perception, aloof with the domination of their desires over them; their intellects, hearts and conduct.

The parent brain knows the results of foolish choices through its experience. And that's why it tries it's best to admonish the child mind. It's been down that road of ignorance and silly behavior which can't be undone. And it only wishes to save the child mind those moments of regrets that it wishes it has been spared. And that's being apparent.

The adult brain which is the parent brain is the conscious one. It's the conservative one who understands that life is not about indulging in every vain desire, it's not about living carelessly or with reckless abandonment. It's the adult in the gathering of minds who is always going to be aware of the threat first before the amusement in every enjoyment or pleasure. It's accountable for the actions that it displayed, which is why its comportment is expressed though safe thinking and considering all possibilities by being smart in the path it takes. It always considers them self as well as other's who will be affected by their actions. It prides its self in making smart decisions and avoiding liabilities or becoming the incapacitate one who keeps screwing up. And though it's sometimes a burden it enjoys being the designated thinker. The one who is always making sure that everyone is responsible or are all secure, accounted for, and are never too rash in their activities.

And I know because all parent brains could relate. By this I wanted readers to know that, not only am I conscious thinker now, but I can truly identify with everything that's said. Because for one, I am the writer. And because I once possessed a child mind. I once made those costly mistakes that has ruin a lot for me. I had to grow up mentally and start using my brain more considerably. My poor choice making caused me a great deal of regret and pain. It cost me an abundance of hurt and suffering that I can never take back. But I knew that I had to change my immature behavior if I ever wanted to stop adding on to all the grief I endured or caused other's. The past error's is always going to be a reminder of what we been through and our insufficiencies, but they don't have to be a reflection of what our future could be. Once a person has gain some understanding it now becomes their duty to teach other's how to think for themselves and those they care for. Though it's not any rewards or ceremonies held for those who actually strive to influence other people lives positively, it's none inquired or ever desired. The duty of a parent brain is not something that is done to seek attention. It's not something done with the expectation of gain. It's something done courteously.

Although the parent brain could be compared to an actual parent, I don't want readers to get the ideal that it's in the sense of having a child. It's not about demanding another person's attention. Or punishing them when they don't listen or defy your commands. It's not about giving birth to a being but giving birth to understanding. It's about being a parent in the sense of being able to raise up an ignorant person from that childish state. It's about clothing them with knowledge and providing the nourishment they minds need to continue to exist without consequences holding them back. It's about guiding the incognizant or providing them with sensible assistance that will help get them through life's vague obstacles.

Personally, I hate to see other's make the unfortunate mistakes that ruin their lives. I hate to see people become a product of their so called environment. A product of something that isn't productive or has been a misguidance. Influencing nothing but failure because they weren't taught to be cautious or heed to advice that's beneficial. So, they're brought and sold because of their incorrect behavior by those who they received these fallacious conceptions from. Whether it's ancestry or those they persuaded by in the streets, because of these mistakes they continually make immaturely. But the parent brain isn't one to complain because he knows what it takes for them to come out of the mind frame. He knows how difficult it is to make that mental transition after being neglectful for so long. But it's more for empowerment and enabling other's to be just as capable. He wants to help every child mind grow up to maintain the same smart thinking he possesses in order for error's to be reduced to a minimum. And that's the acknowledgement of a parent brain.

Black Man Why I Hate My Self

PART THREE

Mirror – Mirror on the wall who is the most racist people of them all?,

I inquired for the third time exhausted by the disturbingly harsh views of the world,

What individual of grave doubt – consternation – or orbit wonder is it who interposed my relaxing state of tranquility while I repose?,

It is I who resembles you that wish to know; I come seeking the truth and desire your advice yet again if it doesn't bother you?,

Oh…It's you again the mirror replied as I stood before my depiction's piercing eye's,
Haven't you learned anything from our observational evaluation?,

Or is your ears deaf to the enlightening information?,

Tell me; what's the point of even having another conversation about the black man's self-preservation in America when you refuse to use your mind instead of keeping it captivated behind the bars of past error's?.

Read between the lines black man,
Redefine who you are in society and take a stance,

Why not risk that chance when many died fighting a struggle for you to live free on this land?,

You'll forever remain in chains of mental enslavement if you don't move forward and utilize past ignorance for future capitalization,

Your lack of progression is deprecating,
You rather hide behind excuses and live in hindrance then to become leader's – role models – or defiant father's who share a king's semblance or reign to uplift a nation,

Years away from the plantation but still you are obedient to its stipulations,

Brain washed to be failures – useless helpers – with no talented abilities,

Have you not witnessed great men accomplishments throughout your history?,

Like I said great men who created once impossible opportunities,

And showed you that your more than a slave trade's commodity or property that was indispensable and incapable of leading society,

But still where's the unity?,
To change is to start believing that you are queens and kings,

And to help one another instead of turning your backs on each other,

Not to be an enemy but an open friend – a supporter – or a brother,

Relieve yourselves of the enmity that resides within,

Embedded in your heads to divide the entire culture crippling your desire to advance,

Restrategize your plans to ascend,

You can no longer pretend to be victimized; it's time for self-pity to end,

Be husbands to your wives instead of the stereotype baby father's leaving women without the support of their lovers who have the nerve to call themselves men?,

Be fathers to your offspring and raise your children to understand equality so they could know what their entitled to and never feel less of a person when their deprived a chance,

Embrace them with love so they'll know the feeling of affection,
And when they are turned away by the world's rejection in your care they will always find acceptance – shelter – and protection,

Teach them that there is no obstacle impossible to achieve,
As long as they believe and stay determined – ambitious – and motivated they'll succeed,

Defeat is just a mind state to keep you impeded while life proceed,

Now black man do you see why the hatred towards your own people is so extreme?,

If you don't take the initiative to gain prosperity; you'll forever be bitter with animosity causing you to be miscreants or dead beats which is obsolete,

Failing in life – love – and fatherhood again and again tediously,

So, answer the calling of your inner selves dying to be helped or forever dwell in pain – misery – and stagnation because you didn't prevail or have the guts to rise to the occasion of uplifting men and women or inspiring children in order to better a nation,

I realized for the first time talking to my reflection that I was my own enemy,

And that I blamed others for my lack of gratification so that the world would have sympathy,

Despising my so-called sister's and brother's,
Disclaiming my own children and deserting their mother's,
Who were once devoted lover's, but my fear of commitment and a unifying existence caused me to feel threatened to devote myself to another,

Threatened because I never knew the feeling of being cohesive or the first thing about family,

Which caused me to be ignorant and sheer from my responsibilities,
But now I see in order to keep this pattern of behavior from remaining the same; that the change I seek has to begin with me,

Or it will continue to be nothing more then complaints in a mirror over a sink which I confide in from time to time looking to find strength and salvation from my own restraints,

Execrable characteristic's and lack of qualities,

Now I leave this mirror in confidence sure to make a difference that's prominent and bring an effective significance to society.

P.O.A.P

Black Man Why I Hate Myself

PART 3

THE BREAK DOWN

This poem is based on the third meeting of a person who for the first time is ready to take heed to the advice he finds deep within himself. That voice that has been neglected before due to his obstinate disregard to see himself as his own enemy. Sometimes we prevent our own conditions or state from bettering because of our failure to adhere to what is obvious. Sometimes we can't begin to find a solution if we refuse to face the most difficult problem which is ourselves. The only true impediment that can stand in the way of our mental awareness. Only then that intuition deep inside of us that wish to correct the dysfunction that impairs our state of reasoning can make the proper adjustments or improvements. The image which is the conscious self begins to instead give unequivocal notification of how he "the self" could refrain from hating his brother's or sister's and improve on this part, rather then provide the answers he's searching for. I also wanted to convey a man's struggle to find questions as to why the hatred that his own people had for each other was so intense. And how a race of people has become so divided and distant from each other to the point of almost being strangers to their own tribe. I wanted to show the lack of leadership – unity – or responsibilities that was causing the black community to suffer. The deficiency in our treatment to women or fatherhood to our children. The neglect of obligations in our duties or positions as black men in this society. The failure to be more laudable and prestigious role models or public figures. The struggle between the conscious mind and the mental unawareness that is seriously affecting the black culture. I wanted to point out everything that has continued to be an excuse to why we as men aren't able to rise from such a hindering state of mind. Everything that is irrelevant to the focus which should be our main concern. My inspiration for this poem came from the thought of wanting to provide our brothers and sisters with a means to change. Wanting them not only to see the problem we face or point out the mistakes we are making as a people but to actually provide a sense of direction in what's needed to be done.

Again, I started this off with the ideal of the person seeking to find answers to a question that continues to bother him. Answers that he has yet to find because of the difficulty he has facing reality. The reality of the true problem being himself and no one else. The mirror reflection is really his consciousness and his heedless self. It's a reflection of who he is but the difference of his awareness and lack thereof. It's the relation of one own self struggling with his identity, his culture, and perspective of his people that just doesn't seem to be practical.

He's aware that his questioning is becoming redundant. He has grown mentally exhausted with these meetings and still haven't found the reason for his self-hatred. This was the third time he came to face himself and wanted answers. He ask finally tired of being given the run around which were excuses he once chose to believe to justify his actions.

It's understood by the conscious state that the grave doubt was the uncertainty of the threat that was causing great harm to his own race. And the consternation came from the fear of changing the way a person view things if there's a problem with their perception. The orbit wonder is the path or sudden change one is considering. The Latin word for orbit is orbita which literally means path. It's understood that there are two parts of the brain. The conscious and the subconscious. Though the conscious has been the one aware of the change that is needed, the subconscious is the one who has prepared a plan to bring about the proper change which is necessary. When the conscious alerts the subconscious of any desire it computes it then manifest a way for the conscious to achieve the desire it seeks. We only have to desire a thing.

The actual person is making it clear that it's him looking deep within himself for clarity. The things he wishes to know are being circulated in his mind and contemplated for a solution. It's the similarity between the thoughts that are pondered upon and the ones that are decided which are the same despite their angle. The self-image which is the heedlessness of a person knows that he had been a constant pest to his conscious state. He knows that he's been agitating and deterrent to the consciences strive to increase its value. And is making it clear that it doesn't wish to waste anymore of its time or be a further irritation.

The conscious is not surprised that this unmindful state is again seeking his advice. It's apparent that everything has to evolve whether it acknowledge it or not. It's the nature of things. But the conscious awareness has grown impatient with this immature way of thinking and is angered with its failure to realize the harm he was causing "himself" (being his people), in their earlier cognizance.

This is a question of self-examination. Many times, we are inattentive to our own instincts, admonishment, or introspection. Sometimes we disregard the thoughts that are conducive to our very own progress or renovation. Are we deaf to enlightening information when it's presented? Do we lack the power or focus to see into a situation and determine how it would affect us? Determine its feasibility to improve our situation especially when it's in good faith? Do we actually know ourselves enough to distinguish the good intentions between the bad intentions we cogitate about?

What's the point of continuing to have these discussions about the black man's self-preservation when it seems they're not taking notice. And what is self-preservation in this case? Is it to maintain one self or to manage as a collective whole? Are we going to continue to confine ourselves to past error's that restrict us from moving forward or are we going to make the necessary modification to cultivate our people? Stop looking for the answers you are making excuses for. Stop accepting a reality that is a figment of your oppression. The answers are clearly in front of you if only you look ahead.

Let's redefine who we are, the way we're perceived, the way we act towards one another, the way we view our brother's and sister's, the purpose we set out to achieve, and take a stance to implement structure, foundation, and unity in our communities or with our people. Why not risk that chance when many have died for the righteous cause for our progression? For us to have an opportunity at living. Why not take that kind of gamble when we are sacrificing our lives to incur our destruction?

We will forever remain in chains. Chains of incarceration, chains of conscious deprivation, chains of a slave mentality, chains of being conditioned to think that we don't deserve better if we don't come together and cohesively rectify this epidemic.

The lack of progression we have been making is disappointing. It's deprecating to see that we are moving backwards instead of the direction it took so much for us to emerge from. We've come so far only to revert to lesser desirability, inferior expedience, and unacceptable suitability. It seems to suit us better to hide behind smoke screens and pretext then to adhere to a responsibility. We find more comfort in a lack of obligation or duty to fulfill a requirement. An imperative necessity to be leaders, role models, and fathers to a nation that is desperate of chiefs. Desperate of the likeness of kings which make excellence and predominant qualities.

Although we're years away from those horrid conditions of those plantations' it seems like we are still obedient to its stipulations. Our weak decisions subject us to punishment and terrible living arrangements due to breaking the law, we are treated and fed like animals, we are forced to labor for pennies and scraps, we leave our sister's and black queens to raise children on their own, we find it hard to commit to one woman, we fail to be father's to our children, and we betray our brother's just to help ourselves. Back during the times of slavery black people were punished daily and given the worse living arrangements to reside. They were treated like animals and only provided enough to barely survive. The men were routed from plantation to plantation to separate families as a punishment and to weaken any chances of hope. They were forces to abandon their responsibilities as a man. They weren't allowed to be fathers to their children to prevent the ideal of raising up strong men. And it was easier to have women raise young men up to be inferior due to their fear of seeing their child brutally harmed. And black men betrayed their brother's back then just to enjoy more comfortable arrangement then they were granted.

We've been told so many times that we'll never amount to nothing. That we aren't capable of great achievement. That we don't serve any purpose. That we shouldn't be here. There are many things said to us to defeat us, to destroy our spirit or discourage us from reaching our full potential, to dissuade us from believing in ourselves, to hinder or dishearten our efforts. But the only way we can actually be deterred is if we accept that we could never be more then what we are told. Look at all the things we accomplished as black people. Look at all the successful things we've come to achieve. It's impossible to believe that we are worthless or insignificant beings. Have we not witness the extraordinary attainments we as black people continue to surmount? Have we to witness the barriers we as black people continue to break down? We've come along way since those times of being known as croppers or farmers. We've come along way from being acknowledged as cotton pickers. Look at all the great men and women who've made it absolutely clear that we could be anything we dream of, from doctors to lawyer's. From astronauts to the president of the united states. There's no excuse to allow ourselves to be defeated by other's perception or impression of us. The limit of what we can do is infinite.

There was a time when we didn't know our measure. There was a time when we didn't believe in ourselves enough to see our range. There was a time when we couldn't vision being anything more then what we were forcefully brought to this country to become. But those great people showed us a way. They made it possible for us to see that we are meant for so much more. How could we not see it for ourselves? We were once viewed as a commodity for slave traders. Stock that was indispensable property. We were never perceived as a people capable of leading society. We were never thought to be a people capable of being creator's, who could innovate, who could help shape this country into so much more. We proved that we can take on such responsibilities with out warrant or consent. So how could we not do more for our own race? How could we let these concerns delude our attention as if it's not a matter that deserves our fight?

Where's the unity? Where's the cohesiveness? Where's the continuity? Why aren't we supportive of each other? Where's the congruity? Why are we rivals to one another? Why aren't we assistive in each other's adversity? Why are we quick to judge, ridicule, or belittle our own people? Why do there have to be motives to our intentions. Why are we so selfish? We must start believing that we have the power to change ourselves and the people around us. We must stop thinking like Indians wishing to be chiefs and start making the decisions that separate us as leader's. Leader's that further us as a group of people and not destroy us due to ignorant judgement or vain desires. We must start believing that we are the kings and queens and provide the best example that's going to influence our people to aggrandize their conditions by seeking better for themselves and other's. We must learn to help each other and not look down on the next person with contempt. Or deny them assistance when they're in need.

We can't wait to see who's going to initiate the invitation of an open friend. We can't wait to see who's going to extend the hand of brotherhood. Someone must make the first move. Someone must take the first step. Relinquish the enmity. Abolish the transgression against each other or people in general. Release the hatred within and let's try to love each other instead for a change. This hatred is crippling our culture. It's dividing our communities and preventing us all form advancing because we as a people could never succeed individually.

Let's rethink our purpose and regroup a more constructive plan that's going to germinate a more productive future for us. We can't continue to play the victim after so many years. We can't continue to allow these poor actions of ours to hold us back as a group and keep us insensibly stagnant collectively.

We must be men. We must step up and adhere to our obligations as father's. We must show our children the responsibility of companionship, commitment, and fatherhood. We must be husbands to our wives and not settle for the typical stereotype baby father. Let's show our women that they are worthy enough to marry the same as they are worthy enough to bed. Let's raise our kids in a stable home where both parents are present and active in there lives instead of leaving women with the accountability to bare alone.

Let's be there for our offspring. Let's guide them the right way and prepare them for the obstacles their up against. Let's show them how to protect themselves by understanding the way the world works and not to expect anything they haven't earned. Let's show them that they can be anything and no matter how hard they struggle to never give up or feel less of a person. Policy makers at last are coming to recognize the connection between the breakdown of American families and various social problems. The folding debate over welfare reform, for instance, has been shaped by the wide acceptance in recent years that children born into single parent families are much more likely that children of intact families to fall into poverty and welfare dependence themselves in later years. These children, in fact face a daunting array of problems. While this link between illegitimacy and chronic welfare dependency now is better understood, policy makers also need to analyze the link between illegitimacy and violent crimes and the parent attachments and violent crime. Without an understanding of the root causes of criminal behavior and how criminals are formed. Urban areas are being torn apart by crime. And without knowledge, sound policy making is impossible to review the empirical evidence in the professional literature of social sciences that gives policy makers insight into the root causes of crime. Over the past 30 years, the rise in violent crime parallels the rise in families abandoned by father's. High crime neighborhoods are characterized by high concentration of families abandoned by father's. State by state analysis by heritage scholars indicates that a 10% increase in the percentage of children living in a single parent home leads typically to a 17% increase in juvenile crime. The rate of violent teens crime corresponds with the number of families abandoned by fathers. But it's not strictly up to policy makers to fix this devastating problem. The root is the fathers who are abandoning these households.

These children need men to show them love so they'll know the feeling of affection and having someone who cares enough to correct their wrong. Show them they're not a mistake and will always have that father figure around so they'll never feel alone or abandoned. Show them your present so that when the world is cruel to them they feel safe enough to know that they have you to protect them. Teach them that there's nothing that can't be done if they put their minds to it. Teach them that whatever they want to do, whatever desire they wish to pursue can be procured if they believe in themselves enough to see it through.

Help encourage their motivation, help inspire their dreams. Teach them perseverance and persistency. Be a reflection of what you want them to be. Be active in how you desire them to reflect you as your progeny. Show them that temporary defeat is just a state of mind and failure only comes when one gives up completely. And by making the effort always allow them a chance to keep up with life's expectations.

Now do you see the importance of our role as black men? Do you actually see the negligence we've been displaying? Do we see how much we are needed? It's honestly an urgency that needs our immediate recourse.

Do we even know why the hatred for our own people is so extreme? Have we ever stop to consider why we despise one another? What could honestly be the reason for our loathe?

If we don't act now and take the necessary steps to flourish as a people and rectify this deficient state we're living in that's causing us to show enmity towards one another, to behave criminally, and display characteristics of an irresponsible adult we'll forever have these impeding problems which are old fashion and a repetitive agitation. Problems that cause us as black people to fail in the area's that are significantly vital to our predominant existence.

Will you not listen to that voice calling out for change? That voice inside you that is begging for you to make a difference to uplift your people instead of ignoring the situation. To correct what's been misguided, misdirected, and misinformed. That voice that sees an urgency to reconstruct the social dysfunction that keeps us in a state of agony and despair. Will you be that inspiration the people need to feel prolific in their endeavors, that motivation women need to feel like their value is truly imponderable, and that influence children need stay resolute in their paths? This is the point where any person standing before a mirror looking deep into his/her soul to find answers, becomes aware of their duties. He/she realizes that they share a reliance to take on an obligation that deserves their unselfishness. It becomes more then the desire for refinement rather then if their actually being personally affected by the problem. This is also where they see that the enemy is the one before the reflection as if they were part of the cause.

Many blame the world for the pleasures they weren't afforded. As do they blame others for their reason of not being fortunate. But what many people don't realize is that until you accept the reality of you own expropriation you would never begin to figure out methods of acquiring those things due your focus being directed at the wrong source for understanding. And sometimes this shift of culpability is intended to draw sympathy when our reasons demand compassion. We sometimes complain so that people would feel sorry for us, for our condition, and what has come to pass. No more sad excuses, no more reproof for the shortcomings we've brought on ourselves, and no more complaints about deprived opportunities we failed to create on our own. Let's change the view we have of our brother's and sister's now that we have this enlightenment. Let's be more assertive in our pursuit for unity.

Let's be the father's our son's and daughter's need us to be. Let's commit ourselves to the responsibility of parenting and partnership.

Let's not continue to let our fear of commitment suppress our role as men. Let's not continue to be threatened by the devotion to be loyal to our women because of past mendacious relationships or trust issues that conflict our emotions. Let's not let the fact that we weren't raised in a functional or stable environment continue to cause us aloofness. Let's not let that be the reason we don't see fit to change the cycle.

The cycle that continues to sheer us away from doing right. The cycle that causes us to blindly follow in ignorance. We see that we could change this pattern of behavior if we see it in ourselves to become a part of the solution that imperatively request our attention. If we don't begin to act, these issues concerning our development wouldn't be nothing more than questions we ask ourselves in a moment of privacy when we're looking to amend the things we most disapprove of when we're searching for clarity.

Poor characteristic's and a lack of qualities could sometimes be the reason for our negligence being that we weren't equipped with a standard of principles that propels us or encourage moral greatness. But we don't have to let it continue to be the future of those we have a chance to save.

Now one should leave this message with an eager confidence to make a difference and bring expedient reform to their community or society in general.

The lesson taught at this point by human experience is simply this, that the man who will get up will be helped up; and the man who will not get up will be allowed to stay down. Personal independence is a virtue and it is the soul out of which comes the sturdiest manhood. But there can be no independence without a large share of self-dependence, and this virtue cannot be bestowed. It must be developed from within.

-Federick Douglas

The Glossary

Abhorrent – Loathsome, Detest

Abolish – To do away with

Abstract – To draw the attention of

Accountable – Responsible, Answerable

Accreditation – Credit

Acquisition – Something Acquired

Acquisitive – Greedy, Eager to acquire

Adamant – Unyielding, Inflexible

Admonish – To warn gently

Adornment – To enhance the appearance of

Advocate – One who pleads another's case

Aggrandize – To make great or greater

Allegory – The expression through symbolism of truths or generalization about human experience

Allocation – To distribute as a shore, to transfer to another

Allured – Charm, Entice

Aloofness – Removed or distant emotionally or physically

Amend – Correction of faults

Amicable – Friendly, peaceable

Amnesty – An act of granting a pardon

Amorously – inclined to love, Being in love

Anguish – Extreme pain or distress

Antipathy – Settled aversion or dislike

Anxiety – Painful uneasiness of the mind

Apostasy – A remunication or abandonment of a former (loyalty as to a religion)

Apprehension – To look forward to with dread

Arbitrary – Determined by will or caprice

Articulate – Expressing oneself readily and effectively

Ascertain – To learn with certainly

Assert – To state positively

Assimilate – To make or become similar, To comprehend

Astray – To go off the right path or route

Atrocious – An atrocious act of object

Attributed – An inherent characteristic

Autistic – A disorder that appears by age three and is characterized esp. by impaired ability to communicate others

Aversion – Something decidedly disliked

Baneful – Poison, Harm, Woe, A source of this

Berate – To scold harshly

Bestow – Put, Place, Stow to present as a gift

Bleak – Lacking warm or cheering qualities

Blunder – Stupid or needless mistake

Bravado – A show of bravery

Buffer – Something that protects or shield

Calamity – Great distress of misfortune

Caprice – An inclination to do things impulsive

Caste   A division in society based on wealth, inherited rank, or occupation

Castigate – To punish or criticize severely

Censurable – The act of condemning sternly

Cessation – A temporary or final ceasing

Chassis – The supporting frame of a structure

Chattel – An item of tangible property, slave, or bondman

Cogent – Having power to compel or constrain

Cognitive – Thinking, Remembering, or reasoning

Cognizance – Notice, heed

Cognomen – Nickname

Comportment – Agree, Accord, Conduct

Compulsive – An irresistible persistent impulse to perform an act

Concur – To act together, to agree

Condemnatory – To declare to be wrong

Conformity – Harmony, Compliance, Obedience

Congruity – Correspondence between things

Conjecture – Guess, Surmise

Consolidation – To unite or become united as a whole

Consternation – Amazed dismay and confusion

Contrast – To show difference when compared

Conviction – The state of being convinced, Belief

Copulation – To engage in sex

Correlation – Establish the mutual relations of

Credulous – Inclined to believe esp. on slight evidence

Culpability – deserving blame

Customary – Commonly practiced of observed

Daunt – To lessen the courage of

Debase – To lower in character or quality

Debauchery – Seduce, Corrupt

Debility – An infirm or weakened state

Decorum – Conformity to accepted standards of conduct

Defamatory – To injure or destroy the reputation of

Delude – Mislead, Deceive

Delve – To seek laboriously for information

Democracy – Government by the people, rule of majority

Deplete – To exhaust of strength or resource

Deprecate   Belittle, to lessen in value

Dereliction – The act of abandoning

Desolate – Desert, Grief, Sadness

Despoiled – To strip of belongings, Possessions or value

Despondent – Hopelessness, Dejection

Devitalize – To deprive of life or vitality

Didactic – Intending to teach or instruct on moral lessons

Differentiate – To make or become different

Diffident – Lacking confidence

Diligent – Characterized by steady, earnest, and energetic effort

Discernment – To distinguish with the eyes

Discourse – Conversation, to express oneself

Disdain – To look on with scorn, to reject

Disembody – To deprive of bodily existence

Disparage – To degrade

Dispiritedness – Depress, Discourage

Dissimulate – To hide under a false appearance

Dissuade – To advise against a course of action

Duplicitous – The disguising of true intent by deceptive words or action

Economical – Operating with little waste

Edification – Instruction and improvement esp. in morality

Elate – To fill with joy

Element – Natural environment

Elite – A superior group

Elucidate – To make clear by explanation

Elude – To escape the notice of

Empirical – Based on observation

Enshroud – To veil or screen from view

Entice – Allure, Tempt

Epidemic – Affecting many persons at once

Epithets – A characterizing and often abusive word.

Equate – To regard or treat as equal

Equity – Justness

Erroneous – Incorrect

Erudition – Learning, Scholarship

Essential – Of utmost importance

Ethical – Principled, conforming to accepted esp. professional standards of conduct

Eulogize – Highly praised

Evasive – An act or instance of evading

Excision – Removed by or as if by cutting out

Excoriate – To criticize severely

Execrable – Very bad

Exonerate – To free from blame

Expedience – A temporary means to an end

Explicit – Clearly and precisely expressed

Expropriate – To deprive of possession or the right to own

Fallacious – Misleading, deceptive

Fealty – Loyalty, Allegiance

Felicitation – Congratulate

Felicity – Something that cause happiness

Filch – To steal furtively

Flare – To become suddenly excited or angry

Flourish – Thrive, Prosper

Foster – To give parental care to, Nurture

Fruitless – Unsuccessful, Not bearing fruit

Germinate – To cause to develop or evolve

Glitz – Extravagant showiness or appearance

Grapple – To seize of hold with or as if a hooked implement

Heinous – Hatefully or shocking evil

Idle – Groundless, Worthless or lazy

Impair – To diminish in quantity, value, excellence or strength

Impecunious – Having little or no money

Immanent – Being within the limits of experience of knowledge

Imperialism – The policy of seeking to extend power, dominion, or territories of a nation

Implausible – Not seemingly worthy of belief

Implicit – Understood though not directly stated or expressed

Imponderable – Incapable of being weighed or evaluated with exactness

Imprudence – Lacking discretion, Wisdom, or Good judgement

Inadvertent – Heedless, Unintentional

Incentive – Something that incites

Incertitude – Uncertainty, insecurity, instability

Inconceivable – Impossible to comprehend

Inculpable – Free from guilt

Indolent – Slow to develop or heal

Inebriation – To make drunk, intoxicate

Inert – Powerless to move, sluggish

Iniquitous   A wicked act

Insalubrious – Unwholesome, Noxious

Insatiable -Incapable of being satisfied

Intangible – Incapable of being touched

Intemperance – Lacking moderation

Introspection – A reflective looking inward

Introvert – A reserved or shy person

Invective – Abusive language or expression

Juxtapose – To place side by side

Lackadaisical – Lacking life, spirit, or zest

Languor – Weak, to become dispirited

Lasciviousness – Lustful, Lewd

Laudable – Praise

Lethargic – Abnormal drowsiness, the quality or state of being indifferent

Lewd – Sexually unchaste

Licentious – Lewd

Malefaction – One who commits an offense against the law

Malefic – Baleful, Malicious

Malignant – Tending to produce death or deterioration

Mendacious – Given to falsehood or deceit

Misconstruction – To misinterpret

Miscreant – One who behaves criminally

Misogynistic – A hatred of women

Monition – Warning, caution

Narcissism – Undue dwelling on one's own self or attainments

Negate – To cause to be invalid

Nocuous – Harmful

Notion – Views, Concepts, Ideals, or Belief

Noxious – Harmful to health or morals

Obscenity – Indecent, Crude, Or repulsive

Obstinacy – Stubborn

Obstruction – Hindrance

Omit – To leave out or leave unmentioned

Omnipotence – Having unlimited authority or influence

Opprobrious – Expression opprobrium, Public disgrace

Optimistic – An inclination to anticipate the best possible outcome

Optimize – To make perfect, Effective, Or functional as possible

Opulent – Richly abundance, wealthy

Ostentation – Pretentious of excessive display

Ostracize – To exclude from a group by common consent

Penury – Extreme poverty

Peonage – One bond to service for payment for a debt

Perplex – To disturb mentally or confuse

Perspicuity – Plain to the understanding

Perturbation – To disturb greatly esp. in mind; Upset

Pessimistic – To expect the worst or take the lease favorable view

Plight – An unfortunate, Precarious, Or difficult situation

Posthumous – Born after death of father, Or published after death of author

Prate – To talk long and idly

Premise – To base on certain assumption

Premonition -Previous warning

Pretentious – Making or possessing usually unjustified claims

Prevalence – Generally or widely existent

Procure – To get possession of, To obtain

Prodigious – Extraordinary in size or degree

Proficient – Well advanced in art, occupation or branch of knowledge

Progeny – Children, Offspring

Prominent – Readily noticeable

Promiscuous – Having a number of sexual partners, Not restricted to one person

Propriety – the standard of what is socially acceptable in conduct and speech

Prudent – Cautious, Discreet

Prurient – Exciting to lascivious

Punitiveness – Involving or aiming at punishment

Ramification – Consequence, Outgrowth

Rash – To hasty in decision, action, or speech; Reckless

Reciprocal – Mutual, Shared

Refinement – Something intended to improve or correct

Reform – To make better or improve by removal of faults

Relinquish – To give up, let go of, or abandon

Remunerate – To pay an equivalent for or to, Compensate

Render – To give in return or to another

Repel – To drive or turn away

Repose – A state of resting, calm, peace

Reproof – Blame or censure for a fault

Repugnance – Strong dislike, Distaste, Or antagonism

Repulsion – A feeling of aversion

Resonate – To relate harmoniously

Rhapsodic – An expression of extravagant praise or ecstasy

Rhetoric – The art of speaking or writing effectively

Roguish – A dishonest or mischievous being

Rubbish – Something worthless, nonsensical

Sacrilege – Violation of something, consecrated to God

Sadism – A sexual perversion in which gratification is obtained by inflicting physical or mental pain on other's

Sadomasochistic – The deviation of pleasure from the infliction of physical or mental pain either on others of oneself

Sagacious – Of keen mind

Salubrious – Favorable to health

Satiate – To satisfy fully or to excess

Servile – Befitting a slave servant, behaving like a slave

Servitude – Slavery, Bondage

Sleuth – Detective

Solace – Comfort, Console

Solemnize – To observe or honor with solemnity

Spouting – to eject or issue forth forcibly and freely

Spurious – Not genuine, False

Strewn – To spread by scattering

Stringent – Strictness, Severity

Subtle – Hardly noticeable

Succinct – Brief, Concise

Sullied – Soiled, Defiled

Sultry – Exciting sexual desire

Suppress – To hold back

Surmise – To form a notion from scanty evidence

Surmount – To overcome

Surreptitious – Done, Made, or acquired by Stealth

Swarthy – Dark in color or complexion

Tarnish – To make or become dull or discolored

Tenacious – Holding fast, Cohesive, or tough

Tenet – One of the principles or doctrines held in common by members of a group (as a church or profession)

Titillate – To excite pleasurably

Torpid – Having lost motion or power or exertion

Transitory – Of brief duration; Short lived

Unctuous – Insincerely smooth in speech and manner

Unequivocal – Leaving no doubt, Clear

Unfetter – Liberate

Un-precedent – Having no Prior in time, order, or significance

Un-scrupulous – Unprincipled

Unwavering – Sound in opinion, direction, or Allegiance

Unwholesome – Harmful to physical, mental, or moral well being

Unyielding – Characterized by lack of softness or flexibility

Vagrant – A person who has no job and wander from place to place

Veracious – Truthful, Honest

Verity – Certainly, in very truth

Vigorous – Done with force and energy

Virtuous – Chaste, Moral virtue

Virulent – Highly infectious, Full of malice

Vital – Concerned with or necessary to the maintenance of life

Vivify – To put life into; To make vivid

Volition – the act or power of making a choice or decision

Vulgar – Lacking Cultivation or refinement

Wholesome – Sound in body, Mind, or morals